FIERY TRAVELS: THE VIA COMBUSTA

Published by My Spirit Books 2012

First published in Great Britain in 2012 by My Spirit Books,
Maidstone TV Studio,
Vinters Park, Maidstone, Kent ME14 5NZ
www.myspiritbooks.com

Cover design by Robert Hammond

Printed and bound in the UK by Biddles, part of the MPG Books
Group, Bodmin and King's Lynn

British Library Cataloguing-in-Publication Data
A catalogue record for this book is available on request from the
British Library

ISBN: 978-1-908810-09-0

CONTENTS

INTRODUCTION

THIS IS THE STORY of a small stretch of sky.

Although it's been known to astrologers for centuries, nowadays only those who favour traditional techniques, or have an interest in astrological history, appear to be aware of it. In modern terms, the Via Combusta is the stretch of the sky between mid-Libra and mid-Scorpio (usually given as 15 degrees Libra to 15 degrees Scorpio).

It tends to be seen as A Bad Thing.

In horary astrology, the Moon in the Via Combusta can indicate a problem with the question. It's also something to be avoided in electional charts. And that is the sum total of most people's knowledge of the Via Combusta.

Astrological writers down the centuries have been extremely reticent about it, seemingly assuming that it's so mind bogglingly obvious what the Via Combusta means that they needn't waste words writing about it.

The Latin term "Via Combusta" is usually translated as "fiery road", "fiery way" or "burnt path". It's common for passages across the sky to be described as roads or paths. Traditionally, the ecliptic is known as the "via solis" and the Milky Way as the "via lactea". Occasionally, the Via Combusta is referred to in Latin texts as the "via adusta" – "singed" path. Or it might be called the "via perusta" – the "scorched path", although this can cause confusion as it's also a term used for the Milky Way. Another term is the "via ignea"– "fiery path", used by Aristotle to indicate

1

comets extending their tail over a great part of the sky.

Astronomically, the Via Combusta lies within the claws of the scorpion – that area of the sky where alchemists believed the Sun needed to be for the transmutation of iron into gold. This accursed constellation was seen as the source of war and plague and at its centre lies the star Antares – the heart of the scorpion.

One of the earliest references to the Via Combusta that we know of is that of Al Biruni's in his *Book of Instruction in the Elements of the Art of Astrology* (from about 1029 CE).

> The combust way is the last part of Libra and the first of Scorpio. These two signs are not congenial to the Sun and the Moon on account of the obscurity and ill-luck connected with them and because each of them is the fall of one of the luminaries. They also contain the two malefics, the one by exaltation (Libra, Saturn) the other by house (Scorpio, Mars). The peculiarity however which has given the name muhtariq is that the exaltation of Saturn is near the fall of the Sun on the one hand and that of the Moon on the other, while the adjacent parts of both signs are occupied by terms of Mars.[1]

Or this is a malefic area of the sky because it contains degrees of the zodiac that are themselves malefic in nature. But how can we be sure? How do we know that these degrees didn't gain a reputation for being malefic *because* they were in the Via Combusta? That this isn't some sort of post-hoc rationalisation by astrologers? The truth is that the Via Combusta is so ancient, we can no longer be sure. But we can explore where the idea of the Via Combusta might have come from and why it endured as a concept for so many centuries.

The Via Combusta is a small stretch of sky. And this is its story.

2

1

LOCATION, LOCATION, LOCATION...

ALMOST ALL OLDER – and traditionally oriented modern – astrological texts mention the Via Combusta, at least in passing. Certainly, those that deal with horary or electional astrology pay it some attention, usually in the context of it being something best avoided. It also appears in medieval texts relating to bloodletting and similar medical activities.

Taking a browse through these texts from practically any era throws up Al Biruni's definition again and again. Although Al Biruni doesn't actually specify the precise degrees, the common view is that it's definitely from 15 degrees Libra to 15 degrees Scorpio. This definition is also given in a variety of older English dictionaries.

> The last 15 degrees of *Libra* and the first 15 degrees of *Scorpio*.[2]

The last 15 degrees of *Libra* and first of *Scorpio*.[3]
Sometimes, its location isn't defined at all, or barely so.

Or the last half of Libra and first of Scorpio.[4]

From the middest of the Signe *Libra* unto the
middest of *Scorpio*.[5]

In general, there seems to be no dispute that the Via
Combusta lies somewhere from the middle of Libra to the
middle of Scorpio – especially when it comes to texts from the
nineteenth century onwards. However, some writers feel that
the area is more expansive. With Scorpio being so malefic,
why stop at half of it when you can have the whole sign?

...in the second half of *Libra*, and throughout the
whole Sign *Scorpio*. All that space is called *Via
Combusta*, the *Combust way*, being about 45
degrees in Longitude.[6]

The space of this half of Libra, and all Scorpio.[7]

Similarly, a few authors are ready to throw the whole of
Libra into the pot as well.

If it is in the burnt path, these are Libra and Scorpio.[8]

This is from Libra to Scorpio.[9]

Simmonite rather excitedly suggests that it may be worth
taking the area to encompass the whole of Sagittarius
and Capricorn while you're at it.[10] On balance, the 15-
15 definition appears to win. Even when there's a slight
change of definition to 14 Libra to 14 Scorpio, it's easy to
attribute that to semantics – perhaps they really meant
"after 14 degrees".

Via Combusta, which is between fourteen degrees of Libra and fourteen degrees of Scorpio.[11]

Francis Barrett, author of the highly influential early nineteenth century *The Magus*, was one of those who favoured the 14-14 definition. No-one would accuse Barrett of originality, but the definitions he chose in general stuck solidly over the next two centuries. So it's a little odd that this one didn't take off. A glance at non-English language sources throws up some anomalies. A fifteenth century Dutch manuscript offers a choice of 13-13, 19-19 and 20-20.

Der Weg im Zodiak zwischen dem 13° der Waage und 13° des Scorpions.
The path in the zodiac between 13° of Libra and 13° of Scorpio.

Ende die verbrande wech begynt vanden 19. grade van Libra ende geduret totten 19. grade van Scorpione.
The burnt way which begins from the 19th degree of Libra and ends at the 19th degree of Scorpio.

...verbranden wech (dat is vanden 20 sten grade van Libra totten 20 sten grade van Scorpione).
The burnt way (which is from 20 degrees of Libra to 20 degrees of Scorpio).[12]

Perhaps that's simply something to do with being Dutch? But then the nineteenth century German astrologer Johannes Vehlow favours 11-11.[13] So what's going on here? Modern (as in post sixteenth century) definitions tend to be of the 15-15 category, with a few exceptions that either favour a wider area or are of a 30 degree band with slightly different start and end points. Earlier references favour associating the start and end points with the degrees of fall of the Sun and Moon.

This is from the dejection of the Sun in Libra to the degree of the dejection of the Moon in Scorpio.[14]

Often, these degrees are specified.

From the 13 degree of Libra, unto the 9 degree of Scorpio, they are likewise infortunate.[15]

On appelle la Voie Brûlée la partie du Zodiaque comprise depuis 13° de la Balance jusqu'à 9° du Scorpion, les planètes en traversant cette région sont dites infortunées.
What is called the Burnt Way is the part of the zodiac between 13 degrees of Libra to 9 degrees of Scorpio, planets crossing this region are said to be unfortunate.[16]

The weakness of a planet is when [it is] in the Fiery Road which is from 19 Libra to 3 Scorpio.[17]

This definition is consistent with that given in the Cairo almanacs of the twelfth century, which were discovered in 1979.[18] It clearly complies with a different demand for tidiness than do the 15-15 and similar definitions. And it's understandable that astrologers would prefer to associate the area's boundaries with degrees that are meaningful to them. Except it isn't clear that this is actually what they were doing.

During the medieval period the 19-3 and similar boundaries are favoured. There are anomalies – Marsilio Ficino favoured another definition entirely:

Burned path from the 28th degree of Libra to the third of Scorpio...[19]
From time to time, you can come across other definitions – 25 Libra to 6 Scorpio, 22-30 Scorpio, the generous 15 Libra to 10 Capricorn ... the list goes on. The wildest seems to be

that offered by Richard Saunders[20] where he suggests 20 Gemini to 1 Cancer in the north parts of the zodiac and in the south from 6 Sagittarius to 16 Sagittarius and from 24 Sagittarius to 5 of Capricorn. He isn't alone – a small number of astrologers cite late Gemini to early Cancer as a possible location, and early twentieth century Russian astrologers place it in late Gemini. There is a reason for this, which will – hopefully – become much clearer in a later chapter. But these definitions are the exception rather than the rule.

It's almost enough to persuade you to take up psychological astrology.

Let's take a quick look at where the Via Combusta is believed to be located over the centuries. I'm not going to attempt to list every occurrence – just some prominent and indicative examples.

Source	♎	♏	Date
Abu Ma'shar	15	15	c.850
Alcabitius	15	15	10th c.
Picatrix	18	3	10th c.
Ibn Ezra	19	3	1147
Cairo almanacs	19	3	12th c.
Bonatus	19	5	13th. c.
Ficino	28	3	15th. c.
Cardan	15	15	16th. c.
Auger Ferrier	15	15	1550
Nicholas Guyer	15	15	1592
Dariot	13	3	1598
John Fage	15	15	1606
William Lilly	15	15	1647
William Ramesey	15	15	1653
John Gadbury	15	15	1658

Source	♎	♏	Date
Joseph Blagrave	15	15	1671
Joseph Moxon	15	15	1679
John Partridge	15	15	1679
Jean Jacques Manget	12	9	1704
John Kersey	15	30	1706
Nathan Bailey	15	15	1737
John Ash	15	30	1754
Francis Barrett	14	14	1801
John Mason Good	0	15	1813
Johannes Vehlow	25	6	1890
WJ Simmonite	15	30 ♑	1890
W Becker	13	9	1930s
Henri Gouchon	13	9	1937
Nicholas de Vore	15	15	1947
Pavel Globa	22	30	
E Kolesova	13	3	

As many astrologers believed the location of the Via Combusta was derived from the positions of a variety of malefic fixed stars, there have been calls to make allowances for precession (for example, Nicholas de Vore suggests moving it along a little).

> A birth Moon in that arc was considered to be as afflicted as if it was in an eclipse condition – at or near one of the Nodes. If so, the

description would have to be revised by one degree every seventy years, to compensate for the precessional arc. This would probably place the Via Combusta in the region occupied by Antares and opposed by Aldebaran, an arc now centering around 10° Sagittarius.[21]

Apart from a few exceptions, there seems to be two approaches to defining the Via Combusta:

• A "let's not get too hung up on exactitude" approach, which places it somewhere from the middle of Libra to the middle of Scorpio.

• A "we really need to be precise and it's probably deeply symbolic" approach, which associated the start and end with the degrees of fall of the Sun and Moon.

If you're an astrologer who enjoys tossing dignities and debilities around (perhaps even hissing words such as "vazarite" under your breath from time to time), the second will make perfect sense to you. In case you aren't, you can take a look at dignities and debilities in the next chapter.

But this approach raises a number of questions. Why should an area of the sky neatly align itself with astrological theory? Or was astrological theory derived from such places in the sky and the phenomena that occurred in them?

And why the anomalies? If almost everyone agrees that the Via Combusta is located from mid Libra to mid Scorpio, what possessed a small number of astrologers to start looking at Gemini and Cancer?

If we can work out what the Via Combusta is and where it originally came from, perhaps we can find the answers to these questions.

2

Averages

I'T'S EASY TO ASSUME that the reason for the location of the Via Combusta being given as 15-15 of the signs concerned is because of a general sloppiness, or a desire to average things out. Similarly, it's easy – for astrologers at least – to assume that the focus on the Moon being there is simply because of the Moon being the fastest moving body to be considered in a chart. However, there is more to it than that.

The first sighting of a Moon was of great importance in ancient times. The end of the lunar month when the Moon disappears from sight is represented in myth as the capture of the Moon by hostile powers. As the precise moment of reappearance could not easily be calculated in the past, a delay in its reappearance could cause great anxiety. Hence the celebrations when the edge of the Moon came into sight. For example, tales are told of shouting, dancing and clapping by nomadic Arab tribes at its first appearance.

The ancient definition of the beginning of the month is debatable as to whether it is the conjunction, or the first invisibility of the old Moon or the first visibility of the new Moon.

The growth of the Moon has long been associated with increase, prosperity and the favourable disposition of the gods. It is followed by a transition to waning strength and power. Therefore, the middle of the month was also an important time and ancient texts are full of references to the exact time when the moon becomes full.

Should the full Moon appear when expected – on the fourteenth or fifteenth day of the month – this would be regarded as favourable. But if the Moon appeared to be full on the thirteenth or twelfth day, or if it was delayed to the sixteenth day, this was a bad omen. The Babylonians held special ceremonies at the middle of the month, which emphasised the hope that the opposition would appear at the right time.

The fourteenth day in particular was seen as unlucky. In fact, the middle of the month was taken to be unlucky or uncertain as it marked a period of transition. The phenomenon of lucky and unlucky days is common in antiquity and elaborate lists exist that show which dates are favourable and unfavourable (these are discussed a little further on). In the Roman calendar the ides (the middle) of every month was seen as inauspicious and it appears that the day named Idus (believed to derive from "iduare", "to divide") originally marked the time of the full Moon. "Beware the ides of March," says the soothsayer to Julius Caesar. (Other lunar phases were also marked as unfavourable and were times when certain restrictions had to be observed, such as fasting, cessation of activity and other forms of abstinence, to avoid arousing the anger of the gods.)

In a number of ancient texts, the designation "shabattum" – believed to be the origin of the term "sabbath" – was applied to the fifteenth day of the lunar month. The Babylonian shabattum does not refer to a day of rest, but rather a day of penance on which an angry deity must be pacified. The Greek calendar also considered the full Moon to mark the middle of the month, as the month began with the evening of which the new Moon appeared. This obviously meant that some months were reckoned at twenty-nine days and others at thirty days, with an intercalary month to bring the year in line with the solar year.

Of course, in such calendars lunar eclipses are only possible at the middle of a month. And if bad things were expected to happen, bringing the prediction in line with a time of month that already promised doom and gloom was only sensible. Modern calendars rely on the solar cycle, rather than the lunar and so the fifteenth day of the month no longer holds the same meaning – we certainly can't rely on it being at the time of a full Moon.

However, the association of the number 15 with the full Moon remains as does the idea of a full Moon heralding a problematic time – assuming you're not a werewolf. So this provides an added reason for the tidy rounding up of numbers we see with the Via Combusta.

3

BEING DIGNIFIED

The most commonly given explanation for why the Via Combusta is located from the end of Libra to the beginning of Scorpio is the one given by Al Biruni, quoted in the introduction to this book. Put simply, the Via Combusta is an area of the sky that starts in a place where the Sun is very weak and ends at a place where the Moon is very weak. As the Sun and Moon are the most important planets to astrologers, and this area contains a number of fixed stars that are believed to have a malefic effect, it makes sense that a planet in this area would be thought of as worrisome at the least.

The strength – or effectiveness – of a planet is measured by a system of dignities and debilities. There are two kinds of dignity – essential and accidental. Essential dignity is the result of the zodiacal degree placement of a planet whereas accidental dignity is concerned with the planet's placement in relation to its house position. Here, we are concerned with essential dignity.

Ptolemy's Table of Dignities

Sign	House	Exalt	Trip. D/N	Terms					Faces			Det.	Fall
♈	♂ D	☉ 19	☉ ♃	♃ 6	♀ 14	☿ 21	♂ 26	♄ 30	♂ 10	☉ 20	♀ 30	♀	♄
♉	♀ D	☽ 3	♀ ☽	♀ 8	☿ 15	♃ 22	☿ 21	♂ 30	☿ 10	☽ 20	♄ 30	♂	
♊	☿ N	☊ 3	♄ ☿	☿ 7	♃ 13	♀ 21	☿ 21	♂ 30	♃ 10	♂ 20	☉ 30	♃	
♋	☽ D/ N	♃ 15	♂ ♂	♂ 6	♃ 13	☿ 20	☿ 21	♄ 30	♀ 10	☿ 20	☽ 30	♄	♂
♌	☉ D/ N		☉ ♃	♄ 6	☿ 13	♀ 19	☿ 21	♂ 30	♄ 10	♃ 20	♂ 30	♄	
♍	☿ N	☿ 15	♀ ☽	☿ 7	♀ 13	♃ 18	☿ 21	♂ 30	☉ 10	♀ 20	☿ 30	♃	♀
♎	♀ D	♄ 21	♄ ☿	♄ 6	♀ 11	♃ 19	☿ 21	♂ 30	☽ 10	♄ 20	♃ 30	♂	☉
♏	♂ N		♂ ♂	♂ 6	♃ 14	♀ 21	☿ 21	♄ 30	♂ 10	☉ 20	♀ 30	♀	☽
♐	♃ D	☋ 3	☉ ♃	♃ 8	♀ 14	☿ 19	☿ 21	♂ 30	☿ 10	☽ 20	♄ 30	☿	
♑	♄ N	♂ 28	♀ ☽	♀ 6	☿ 12	♃ 19	☿ 21	♄ 30	♃ 10	♂ 20	☉ 30	☽	♆
♒	♄ D		♄ ☿	♄ 6	☿ 12	♀ 20	☿ 21	♂ 30	♀ 10	☿ 20	☽ 30	☉	
♓	♃ N	♀ 27	♂ ♂	♀ 8	♃ 14	☿ 20	☿ 21	♄ 30	♄ 10	♃ 20	♂ 30	☿	☿

The essential dignities are rulership, exaltation, triplicity, term and face. The more dignity a planet has, the stronger it is. Debility is the opposite of dignity. The debilities are those places where a planet is weakened. The debilities are detriment (opposite to rulership) and fall (opposite to exaltation).

By using this system, astrologers can judge the relative strengths of the planets in a chart. They can additionally interpret a planet placed in a positive or negative zodiacal area as offering a positive or negative answer to a question in horary astrology. Or positions can be avoided, or sought out, when casting an electional chart. The system of dignities and debilities is traditionally taken into account in all fields of astrology.

Rulership is the strongest dignity. Except for the Sun and Moon, each planet rules one sign by day and one by night. (A planet without any essential dignity is considered weakened and is called "peregrine".) The system of rulership we know today however isn't the only one that has been used in astrology. The month gods pre-date planetary rulers of the signs of the zodiac and appear in Egyptian art as early as the eighteenth dynasty, about 1600 BCE. The Romans associated an Olympian with each month as a tutela or guardian. The tutela were twelve, six male and six female and the period of October/November was ruled by Mars. (Modern astrology offers each planet one sign of rulership in order to accommodate the outer planets.)

Mercury is the only planet with the same sign for his exaltation as his rulership. Exaltations were often assigned to particular degrees in ordinal numbers (for example, Jupiter to the fifteenth degree of Cancer). In Vedic astrology, the level of exaltation varies throughout the sign.

Because the Moon's nodes are markers on the ecliptic rather than bodies, they tend to be ignored in the Western astrological tradition and are not always included in this system. Al Biruni points out that Hindu astrologers in his time did not recognise the exaltations of the nodes – a principle he described as being "quite proper".[22]

However, later Indian astrologers did allocate dignity to the nodes – usually the north node is exalted in 3° Gemini and the south node in 3° Sagittarius. This is the same as given by Rhetorius around the end of the sixth century. Although some authorities have suggested other dignities for the nodes, these aren't generally accepted. Additionally, the exaltations of the nodes aren't always consistent – Taurus and Scorpio are given in Maharishi Parashara's *Brihat Parashara Hora Sastra*, a primary text for Vedic astrologers.

Although there is a great deal of consistency over the centuries when it comes to the dignities, there are differing versions of the terms. Ptolemy in his Tetrabiblos describes three systems – the Egyptian, Chaldean and an ancient system he discovered in a manuscript, or the system that has come to be named after him. Most astrologers in Hellenistic times appeared to have used the Egyptian terms. Ptolemy's terms became more popular from the Middle Ages to the seventeenth century. Although there are differences between the systems in how large the bounds are, they share common features. The Chaldean system allows for a diurnal or nocturnal birth, with the term positions of Saturn and Mercury dependent on this and is different to the other systems in that it has a regular division of degrees in each sign. (The first term always has 8 degrees and each succeeding term one degree less (8-7-6-5-4).)

When it comes to considering the Via Combusta, the relevant terms are:

Egyptian	21° ♎ ♀	28° ♎ ♂	7° ♏ ♂
Ptolemaic	19° ♎ ☿	24° ♎ ♂	6° ♏ ♃
Chaldean	26° ♎ ♀	0° ♏ ♂	8° ♏ ♃

Whichever system we consider, the last few degrees of Libra and the first few of Scorpio are under the rulership of Mars.

Many astrologers adopted a systematic approach to chart analysis by assigning numerical scores based on dignifying or debilitating factors. Al Biruni mentions that this was common amongst the Babylonians and Persians, and the practice continues well into the seventeenth century with, for example, William Lilly giving a detailed table of scoring factors in his *Christian Astrology* of 1647.

The practice of comparing the totals of each planet in order to discover which was most eminent in the chart resulted in the almuten (from the Arabic al-mateen, meaning "firm one" or "strong in power") or lord of the geniture (or nativity), which would be given particular consideration for its powerful influence.

The explanation given for why the Via Combusta is seen as malefic is a combination of:

Saturn is exalted in Libra (21 degrees)
Mars is the ruler of Scorpio
The Sun is in fall in Libra (19 degrees)
The Moon is in fall in Scorpio (3 degrees)
25-30 Libra is in the terms of Mars
0-6 Scorpio is in the terms of Saturn
0-10 Scorpio is in the face of Mars
Mars is in its own triplicity in Scorpio

In other words, the two lights, the Sun and Moon, are weak, while the two traditionally evil planets, Saturn and Mars, are strong.

In addition, this area of the zodiac is also associated with a number of fixed stars seen as malefic, in particular Antares – the heart of the scorpion.

Medieval astrologers defined the Via Combusta as stretching from the eighteenth degree of Libra to the third degree of Scorpio, which suggests that the Sun was exalted in the eighteenth rather than the nineteenth degree of Aries while the Moon appears from under its beams precisely fifteen degrees away, by direct motion (vazarite) in the third degree of Taurus.

If Al Biruni is correct and the Via Combusta simply marks an area of the sky that is outlined by weak positions for the Sun and Moon, then to be able to date the origin of the Via Combusta, we need to know how old the system of exaltations is. The problem is that there is no consensus on this issue.

The oldest of the dignities is exaltation. Rulerships can be seen in our oldest extant Greek horoscopes and triplicities were derived from the rulerships and exaltations – they were used extensively in medieval astrology. Faces are also known as decanates or decans and originate in the ancient Egyptian calendar, which divided the year into 36 ten-day periods each presided over by a particular stellar deity. They are known to have been important in late Egyptian astrology and date back to at least 150 BCE. (In the past, faces were used extensively in weather forecasting.)

It is generally considered that the exaltations date back to ancient Mesopotamian astrology from an era which pre-dates the earliest known use of the zodiac. As the system is found in the tradition of *Enuma anu enlil*,[23] its roots may extend into the last centuries of the second millennium BCE.[24] It's unknown why the Babylonians considered these placements to be dignified, although there are plenty of theories.

Cyril Fagan speculated that the planets all rose heliacally at these degrees in the year of the erection of an important temple to the Babylonian god Nabu in the year 786 BCE. It's true that most of the planetary exaltations have remained very close to the degrees of their heliacal phenomenon in 786 BCE, but the position's don't represent an actual chart for the foundation or opening of the temple as Mercury can't be in Virgo while the Sun is in Aries. They are simply heliacal phenomena recorded during that year.[25]

Why this particular year should be at the base of the system of exaltations is unclear. Rupert Gleadow postulated that the genesis of Nabu came to mimic the essence of the Egyptian Sothic calendar and that when the Chaldeans increased in numbers and power in the sixth and fifth centuries BCE, Nabu became more and more of an icon for that society's roots, and therefore the astrology of that year became very important as well.

> Exaltation] translated means in fact 'hiding-places', and the hiding-places of a planet are obviously those parts of the zodiac in which it is invisible, and especially the degree in which it disappears from view into the sun's rays at heliacal setting and the degree of its reappearance at heliacal rising. The same is true of the moon, and is proved by the distance of the moon's 'hiding place' from the sun's, 14°, which is a typical elongation for a new crescent. Since these phenomena change their positions every time they occur, we are evidently faced by an historical date, and there can be no doubt whatever that this date is 786-785 BC. As for the sun having a hiding-place, it emerges from darkness at dawn on New Year's Day.[26]

Exaltations are believed to be one of the few techniques that were directly inherited and incorporated into the Hellenistic system from the Mesopotamian tradition, as well as one of the oldest techniques that survives to this day.

> Hellenistic exaltations are thought to be the equivalent of the Mesopotamian bit nisriti, or

'secret houses' and this association has been common place amongst academics since the second decade of the 20th century. Indeed, even the 4th century astrologer Firmicus Maternus says quite explicitly that the Hellenistic exaltations were derived from the earlier Mesopotamian tradition, and this statement is sometimes cited as an admission of the transmission of this concept to the Hellenistic tradition.[27]

A problem is that in each of the existing Mesopotamian charts where the "secret houses" are mentioned, and specific planets are said to be in their own "secret house", the signs mentioned don't match the Hellenistic exaltations. Although some cuneiform sources provide evidence for such a connection, these sources are mostly dated to well within the Hellenistic period, leading to the possibility that the transmission could be going in the other direction and that the Hellenistic exaltations were developed separately. Another view is that the pattern derives from the cross of the solstices and equinoxes.

Jupiter and Mars, the most beneficial and malevolent planets, are located close to the stars that, by their rising, mark the summer and winter solstices respectively. On the equinoxial arms of the cross, Saturn occupies a position close to the autumn equinox, and opposite it, at the station of the New Year, are the Sun and Moon. The Sun marking the spring equinox proper while the Moon occupies its ideal calendrical position at the start of the year.[28]

Unfortunately:

The Exaltations of Mercury and Venus are a

little more problematic as they don't fit into the solstice-equinox pattern.[29]

A more recent theory is that of Joanne Conman,[30] who speculates that the exaltations are derived from specific Egyptian decan stars that were venerated in Middle Kingdom Coffin Texts from about c. 2000 BCE and that they survived in later Babylonian astrological texts to become the corresponding planetary exaltations (or hypsomata) of Hellenistic astrology. This would date them back long before anything like this is attested in Mesopotamia.

The apparent consistency of exaltation degrees – which we need if the Via Combusta is to be defined by them – doesn't actually exist, as Al Biruni pointed out.

> There is no difference of opinion as to the signs of exaltation, but the Hindus differ as to the degrees in certain cases. They are agreed that the exaltation of the Sun lies in 10° of Aries, of Jupiter in 5° of Cancer, of Saturn in 20° of Libra...[31]

This may be due to an attempt to update the traditional zodiac positions in response to the effect of precession. As in Hellenistic and Vedic astrology aspects were generally recognised from sign to sign, we don't know whether the distance of a planet from the exact degree of exaltation had much significance. However, the degree itself was certainly used by some ancient astrologers.

Mathematical explanations have been offered for why specific degrees are associated with exaltations:

> The Sun received exaltation in 19 degrees Aries because the entire zodiac consists of a 360-degree circle and the square root of 360 is 19. The exact exaltation is at 18AR56.[32]

What we are certain of is that the use of systems of dignities is certainly very ancient and much older than Ptolemy's scheme and he was responsible for amalgamating them into what he saw as a consistent system. There is certainly elegance to the system. Porphyry[33] points out that all of the diurnal planets have their exaltations in signs which are configured to one of their rulerships by trine, while the nocturnal planets have their exaltations in signs that are configured to one of their rulerships by sextile.

And Robert Schmidt has pointed out that when the exaltation signs of the planets are superimposed on the Thema Mundi, they all fall in signs that are configured to the ascendant, which is in Cancer in the Thema Mundi.[34]

THEMA MUNDI

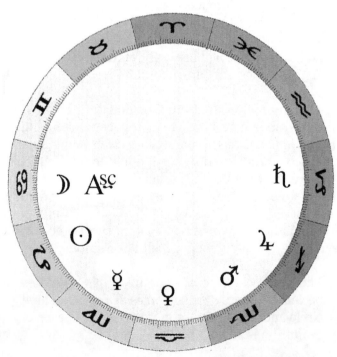

All positions 15°

The Thema Mundi (World Chart) was a horoscope used in Hellenistic astrology that supposedly showed the positions of the seven visible planets (including the Sun and Moon) at the beginning of the universe. Firmicus Maternus (in the fourth century CE) uses an "Egyptian" system, which says the planets are at home in the signs they occupied when the Demiurge created the world.

There have been several creation charts. Indian astrology based calculations on a year in which Sun, Moon, planets and nodes (Lunar and planetary) were said to coincide in 0° Aries. Kepler mentions a creation chart with Sun, Mercury, Venus North lunar nodes in 0° Libra and Mars, Jupiter and Saturn in 0° Aries while the Moon was placed in 0° Capricorn. Paul of Alexandria describes a thema mundi with the Sun at the 19th degree of Aries – its exaltation degree.

All versions have Cancer rising with the Moon in Cancer and the vast majority with the Sun in Leo and the rest of the visible planets fanning out in zodiacal order based on their relative speed and distance from the Sun. One reason given for Cancer rising is given by the third century BCE Mesopotamian astrologer Berossus, who stated that all of the planets conjoined in Cancer indicates the destruction of the world by a great flood, and when they all conjoin in the sign Capricorn it was said to indicate the destruction of the world by fire.

The Thema Mundi goes part way towards explaining why 15 degrees of the signs were used to define areas such as the Via Combusta. Rather than being an actual chart however, it is a diagram used to teach how to read a chart.

When it comes to the oft stated theory that the Via Combusta is marked by the degrees of fall of the Sun and Moon – Houston, we have a problem. Although the degrees of the exaltations have remained consistent for centuries, they have not always been accepted to be where we now know them.

The Babylonian cuneiform tablet VAT 7851 shows the Moon at exaltation in conjunction with the Pleiades (as it is in Hindu tradition) – at 5 degrees of Taurus. (Similarly, Jupiter is exalted at 12½ degrees of Cancer and Venus in Leo.)

What is also apparent is that the Moon had an exaltation degree before the zodiac was reduced from the Babylonian eighteen signs to its current twelve signs. In other words, it's likely that exaltations pre-date the zodiac.

Therefore, although, from wherever it was derived, the elegant system of dignities and debilities described above cannot be assumed to be what gives us the Via Combusta, although it's obviously possible that the fine tuning was done to fit the Via Combusta more comfortably into the astrological system.

So far, we've looked at the idea that the Via Combusta is a bad area of the sky because of the debilities defined in astrological theory.

But perhaps it's the other way around?

Something bad could have led to this area of the sky being marked in such a way. This event could have been at the basis of exaltations. And if we look back at this area of the sky over the centuries, we can begin to understand why it has such a bad reputation.

4

Give me a Sign

When wondering why the Via Combusta crosses the boundary between two signs (admit it, you were wondering), it's worth remembering that Libra is a comparative latecomer to the zodiac, while Scorpio is one of the oldest constellations known – possibly even one of the original six signs of the zodiac – and was well established by 4000 BCE, if not before.

The zodiac belt extends from the ecliptic – the great circle that marks the Sun's apparent path around the Earth. It takes its name from the eclipses that occur in the joining of the Sun and Moon on this path. The constellations along the ecliptic provide a useful backdrop against which the movements of the planets can be tracked.

There is a long standing myth that the twelve sign zodiac dates back to prehistoric times – six thousand or more years ago. However, the antiquity of the zodiac has been challenged since the early twentieth century and it's now generally believed that it originated in Mesopotamia no earlier than the first millennium BCE. It appears that the zodiac is Babylonian (Mesopotamian) in origin and that it evolved slowly during the period 1300 BCE to 500 BCE.

The scheme of Babylonian constellations was established in the second millennium BCE to mark three stellar paths – those of Anu, Enlil and Ea the three most important Babylonian gods. Some constellations that later formed part of the zodiac were established around 2000 BCE (or perhaps earlier). There may also have been earlier Sumerian constellations.

There was a significant change in Babylonian astronomy around 1000 BCE with the Mul.Apin series, which established the preconditions for the establishment of the zodiac. Before the Mul.Apin, astrolabes and star lists were drawn to show which stars were visible in the sky at the different seasons of the year. Astrolabes were circular devices that arranged the stars into three paths that trisected the sky at the eastern horizon. The central segment contained much of the constellations Pisces, Aries, Taurus and the Pleiades. The northern path held Cancer, Leo and Ursa major and the southern Scorpio, Sagittarius, Capricorn and Aquarius. This three-sectioned wheel was subdivided into twelve sections, allowing the months of the year to be identified with the rising of particular stars. The oldest surviving astrolabe was written in Assur around 1100 BCE.

The Mul.Apin "stars of the plough" was discovered in the library of King Ashurbanipal, ruler of Assyria between 669-626 BCE. It is our oldest detailed catalogue of the constellations, and a compilation of all the astronomical knowledge available to the Mesopotamians before the seventh century BCE. An existing copy has been dated to 687 BCE, although it is known to be a reproduction of an earlier text presumed written around 1000 BCE.

The path of the Moon was described on the first Mul.

Apin tablet, giving seventeen (or eighteen, depending on how the list is interpreted) asterisms (the basis for the lunar mansions).

The second table described the path of the Sun and shows that the solar year was divided into a scheme of twelve months of thirty days each, during which the sun occupied different parts of the sky. The year was divided into four seasons and each of these seasons divided into three solar months.

Before the Mul.Apin system, the ecliptic was not specifically identified in Babylonian astronomy. Not all of the constellations used to mark the path of the Moon were within the ecliptic. However, these constellations were to form the basis of the twelve constellation solar zodiac.

The eighteen constellations were introduced in the series as: "the gods standing in the path of the Moon, through whose domain the Moon passes every month and whom he touches":

1. Mul Mul "stars/hairbrush" (Pleiades)
2. Gud Anna "bull of heaven/bull of Anu" (Taurus)
3. Siba Zi Anna "shepherd of heaven/shepherd of Anu" (Orion)
4. Shi Gi "old man" (Perseus)
5. Zubi "scimitar/hooked staff" (Auriga)
6. Mastabba Galgal "great twins" (Gemini)
7. Al Lu "crab" (Cancer)
8. Ur Gul La "lion/lioness" (Leo)
9. Ab Sin "furrow/barley stalk" (Virgo/Spica)
10. Zibanitu "scales/horn" (Libra)
11. Gir Tab "scorpion" (Scorpius)
12. Pa Bil Sag "grandfather/name of a god" (Sagittarius)
13. Suhur Mas Ku "goat-fish" (Capricorn)
14. Gula "great one/giant/great star" (Aquarius)
15. Kun Mis "tails" (Pisces)

16. Simmah " great swallow" (SW Pisces and Epsilon Pegasi)
17. Mul Anunitum "goddess Anunitum" (NE Pisces and centre of Andromeda)
18. Lu Hunga "Hired Man" (Aries)

The "tail of the swallow" (Pisces) has also been read as two constellations, "the tail" and "the swallow", hence the uncertainty whether the "zodiac" consists of seventeen or eighteen constellations.

In about 700 BCE a "zodiac" of twelve irregular sized constellations had been developed of groupings that were nearest to the path of the ecliptic. Only the twelve asterisms closest to the path of the ecliptic were used.

A Babylonian text from the fifth century BCE which lists twelve months (ignoring the intercalary month) assigns both the Pleiades and Taurus to month 2, Orion and Gemini to month 3 and both Pegasus and Pisces to month 12, showing another step towards the twelve sign zodiac.

Around 420 BCE the Babylonians substituted the original twelve constellations forming the zodiacal scheme with a sidereal scheme of twelve equal divisions of the ecliptic comprising 30° segments. Measuring bodies against the background stars had a number of disadvantages – including obscuration of the stars by mist and the difficulty in distinguishing constellation boundaries. A mathematically devised system allowed for greater precision in recording planetary movement.

A number of different reasons lay behind the selection of a twelve sign zodiac, astrolabes had long been dividing the heavens into twelve parts to aid an association between astronomical conditions and the twelve lunar months of the solar year and allotting 360° to the area meant that each sign measured exactly 30°, even though the constellation figures they were named after varied. (The Babylonians didn't see the zodiac as a circle however, but as a band.)

The zodiac of twelve equal signs was never used by the Babylonians as a coordinate system but as a mathematical abstraction for computing lunar and planetary motion. The Normal Stars (a set of approximately thirty stars positioned around the ecliptic) continued to be used for locating the positions of the Moon and planets. The Babylonians discarded the old reference system of the three paths at this time.

The Babylonians defined the starting points of the scheme of zodiacal signs by their positions relative to the fixed stars. For reasons unknown, the completed zodiacal system of the Babylonians did not start at $0°$ ecliptic longitude but at about $355°$ and this difference extends through the whole zodiac.

It's hard to precisely identify Babylonian constellations and we can't assume that they match our modern zodiac signs. However, the scales are mentioned in the Stars of Elam, Akkad, and Amurru (circa 1350 BCE) and appear on an astrolabe from circa 1150 BCE, as well as in the Mul.Apin.

The zodiac we use today is based on that of the Greeks. This is shown to have been formalised by the latter half of the fifth century BCE when the Greek astronomers Meton and Euctemon used it in their star calendars based on a division of the year into zodiacal signs.

Some Greek constellations were established earlier. Homer (circa 750 BCE) in his epic poems the Iliad and Odyssey mentions six constellations and the star Sirius. Hesiod in his poem Works and Days names almost the same constellations as Homer. The Greeks located the beginnings of the zodiacal signs differently to the Babylonians and changed the Babylonian zodiacal constellation the "hired man" into Aries. Aries was incorporated into the Mesopotamian zodiac after the conquest of Egypt by the Assyrians in 671 BCE. Later, the Romans later reintroduced the Babylonian zodiacal constellation Libra.

Libra had been included in the Babylonian zodiac, but was later described by Hellenistic astronomers, such as Ptolemy, as the claws of Scorpio. Evidence suggests that the Babylonian constellations which were to form the final zodiacal twelve were formulated into a zodiacal scheme in about the seventh century BCE. Although there is no mention of the zodiacal scheme in Babylonia (or elsewhere in the Occident) before the first millennium BCE, some constellations that later formed part of the zodiac were established in Mesopotamia by about 2000 BCE. Although eight of our twelve present zodiacal constellations existed in the second millennium BCE there were at least four constellations – that were to form part of the zodiacal scheme – that most probably did not exist until the first millennium BCE.

Around the sixth century BCE there were eleven zodiac signs. Anaximander (d. 546-545 BCE), Cleostratus and Oenopides of Chios (second half of the fifth century BCE) all recognised the eleven sign zodiac.

Accounts exist of a change from a ten month to a twelve month at the time that the zodiac changed – the naming of our months hints at this, – our last four months in Latin are Septem, Octem, Novem, Decem or seven, eight, nine and ten.

The rationale for having ten divisions is that there were originally two separate standards (solar and lunar) used to the measure the months, years, and seasons. The solar year comprised ten months of thirty-six days each, with five days sacred to the gods. The lunar year consisted of thirteen months of twenty-eight days each, with one day left over

There has been plenty of speculation about who was responsible for reforming the zodiac into its current twelve sign form. The theosophists would like us to believe that Samothracian priests held a committee meeting and came up with the idea.[35]

Cleostratus of Teneddos (ca. 520 BC; possibly 548 BC to 432 BC) the author of an astronomical work called *Astrologia* or *Phaenomena* has been credited with having introduced the zodiac (beginning with Aries and Sagittarius according to Pliny) and the solar calendar to Greece from Babylonia. Alternatively, Oenopides of Chios (second half of the fifth century BCE) has also been given credit.

When the tropical zodiac was introduced, the point of the Vernal Equinox was not firmly established but variously placed among the early degrees of Aries. Older authorities placed it at the fifteenth degree. (This would allow the association of the fifteenth degree of Libra as the area of the Sun's seasonal death at the autumn equinox.)

It appears to have been Hipparchus of Rhodes (second century BCE) who first redefined the boundaries of the twelve signs so that the vernal equinox was placed at the beginning of the (Greek) sign of Aries and this now became the starting point for the zodiacal division of twelve equal signs. This system replaced the zodiacal scheme of visible constellations. Claudius Ptolemy (in the second century CE) consolidated this system to get rid of the inconvenience of precessional movement and confusion regarding the sidereal and tropical zodiacs. When the tropical zodiac was introduced, the point of the Vernal Equinox was not firmly established but variously placed among the early degrees of Aries. Older authorities placed it at the 15th degree. This would allow the association of 15th degree of Libra as the area of the Sun's seasonal death at the autumn equinox.

Early Greek astronomers described what we now know as Libra as the "Claws of the Scorpion". Geminus (about 80 BCE) appears to be the first Greek who distinguishes the seventh sign as Libra (Ζυγός) a term used by Ptolemy, who treats the fixed stars of Libra as the "Claws of the Scorpion" (Χηλαί), although he also speaks of Libra when referring to the properties of the sign as a whole.

The term "Libra" was first formally adopted by the

Romans in the calendar of Julius Caesar formed in 46 BCE to whom it may have been suggested by Sosigenes, the astronomer from Alexandria. Vitruvius, Columella, and Pliny distinguish this sign by the name Libra alone. Others use either Libra or Chelae (claws) while Manilius combines both into one phrase. The Mesoptamians referred to this area as the "horns" of the Scorpion.

In the commentary of Theon on Ptolemy's *Almagest*, Libra is frequently represented by "Litra" or "Litrai", a word originally borrowed by the Romans from the Sicilians that was later transformed into "Libra".

The sign of Scorpio itself is extremely old and has been found on Babylonian boundary stones dating to the twelfth century BCE. The name of Scorpio has remained reasonably consistent since Greek times. (Σκορπιός), although Cicero, in his translation of Aratus, and Manilius, also use the term "Nepa" a word of African origin, sometimes employed to denote a scorpion and sometimes a crab, which is why Cicero indicates the fourth sign by the word *Nepa*.[36]

In ancient Mesopotamia, Scorpio was viewed as a symbol of darkness and resilience, due to the decline of the Sun's power after the autumnal equinox, then located within its stars. The main star of the constellation, Antares, is one of the most easily identifiable stars in the sky. At the centre of Scorpio, Antares is also known as Cor Scorpii (Heart of the Scorpion) or the "fire star'" owing to its notable red colour. Antares was one of the four royal stars of Persia, the "Watcher of the West" and a number of early Grecian temples were oriented towards the rising or setting of Antares at the equinox.

The Akkadians called Scorpio "Girtab", meaning the seizer or stinger, and "place where one bows down." Some early translators of cuneiform texts rendered its name, "the double sword." Aratus referred to it as the "great beast' and the "great sign", acknowledging the larger size of Scorpio. The ancient Persians called it Kazhdum, meaning "scorpion" or "scorpion-monster".

In astrology, Antares offers extremes of success, good fortune, danger and malevolence, as well as having the potential for great power.

A number of stars in Scorpio traditionally have malefic qualities. Graffias is a triple star located on the head of the scorpion. Its name originates from the word for "crab", the term for the two creatures being almost interchangeable in early cultures. In some lists it is given as Akrab, Frons Scorpii or "Crown of the Forehead". According to Ptolemy it is of the nature of Mars and Saturn and it is mentioned by Robson as causing "extreme malevolence, mercilessness, fiendishness, repulsiveness, malice, theft, crime, pestilence and contagious diseases".

Isidis, near the right claw, is also attributed a nature like Mars and Saturn and is associated with imprisonment and shame, disgrace and assaults. The stars in the sting of the Scorpion are notorious for causing blindness and injuries to the eyes.

Lesath, in the sting of the Scorpion, derives its name from the Arabic Al Las'ah, "the sting" and has the nature of Mercury and Mars. Traditionally, it's an unfortunate and unlucky star, reputed to bestow danger, violence, immorality and an affiliation with poisons.

Aculeus and Acumen are twin nebulas in the sting of the Scorpion, both likened to the nature of Mars and the Moon. They have a reputation for blindness, sickness and disease.

Not only are the boundaries of the Via Combusta unclear (without even considering such issues as precession) the location of the signs it falls in have shifted over the centuries. However, Scorpio – especially as a double sign – is one of the most ancient signs of the zodiac and the areas of the sky it has covered have long been thought to be malefic. The origin of the Via Combusta could easily be prior to that of the zodiac we know today.

5

SHOOTING STARS

Comets make an impressive sight nowadays, and in the times before light pollution they would have been breath takingly magnificent.

The sight of a comet could last days or even weeks. It was common to view the appearance of a comet as an omen and therefore many early cultures kept detailed records of sightings. Seemingly independent of the Sun, Moon or planets, a comet would trace its path across the heavens with its tail unfurling across the sky, pointing to the west when seen in the morning and the east at night.

We now know that comets are made up of ices of ammonia, hydrocarbons, water and carbon dioxide that bind together pieces of meteoritic stone. They aren't actually very large, averaging approximately a few tens of kilometres in diameter. The increase in comet activity takes place when it's near to the Sun, causing its tail and head to appear. The tail always points away from the Sun, and the head is the nucleus plus a ball of dust and gas left as the comet vaporises. Comets have two types of luminous tails – a straight one is made of gas and a curved tail is made up of tiny particles of dust.

Comets release particles via their tails. If the Earth passes through the comet's tail, the particles burn up as they enter our atmosphere. These are seen to be shooting stars – meteors. A piece of matter as small as a grain of sand can form a meteor, while one that is the size of a grape will create a fireball, which can cast shadows. (If a piece of this rock actually manages to survive to hit the ground, then it is called a meteorite. As comets travel they are subject to gravitational forces that can alter the shape and length of their orbits and cause the comet to disintegrate.

Identifying the precise nature of phenomena in ancient times and early history is difficult – the imagery and vocabulary used to describe it varies depending on when and where the sighting took place. Therefore, supernovae (cataclysmic explosion of a star) and other phemomena could fall within the description of a comet.

It was the Greeks who made the first steps to understanding comets – the word "comet" is derived from the Greek for "long-haired star". Democritus (ca.460 BCE–ca.370 BCE) thought that comets were produced when one star passed near to another. (Not too inaccurate given that we now know about the Oort cloud and the subtle gravitational tugs that can precipitate a cometary event.)

Unlike the Babylonians and Chinese, the ancient Greeks don't appear to have kept detailed records of daily phenomena and they drew mainly on Babylonian records for the data they used in their theories.

Western beliefs about comets were influenced for more than two thousand years by the Greek philosopher Aristotle, who declared in the fourth century BCE that comets were strictly atmospheric phenomena. According to Aristotle, comets were produced by gases that rose into the upper atmosphere where they caught fire, apparently being ignited by sparks generated by the motion of the heavens around the Earth. If the gases burned quickly, they produced the sudden flash of a shooting star. If they burned slowly, a comet was the result.

Not everyone shared this view. Lucius Seneca, a Roman of the first century CE, argued that comets were celestial bodies moving on orbits like planets and that they might reappear, given time.

Aristotle's ideas were finally challenged in 1577 when Tycho Brahe collaborated with other astronomers across Europe. Observations found none of the parallax that would have been evident had comets been as close to Earth as Aristotle predicted.

One event that affected ideas relating to the nature of comets in ancient Greece was the fall of a meteor in 467/6 BC. At the time of the meteor, a comet was visible – possibly Halley's Comet.

The Aegospotami meteorite fell in broad daylight and was recorded as being as large as a wagonload. People still could observe it in the time of Pliny (23-79 CE), about 550 years after the fall. According to Damaichus of Plataea, who lived in the fourth century BCE, a very large fiery body was observed in the heavens for seventy-five days continually *before* the Aegospotami stone fell to earth.

Plutarch later wrote that it was:

> ...like an inflamed cloud, not still but moving with complex and branching motions, so that fiery fragments from its shaking and errant course flew in every direction, flashing like shooting stars.[37]

A meteorite could not have been visible in the skies for seventy-five days, so it seems likely that it was accompanied by a comet. On 4 June a conjunction of Venus, Jupiter, and the Moon occurred at sunset. Halley's Comet could have become visible soon after near the Pleiades – opposite the Via Combusta.

The Aegospotami meteorite influenced the theories of Anaxagoras (500-428 BCE.) and Diogenes (412-323 BCE). Anaxagoras had supposedly used his theories to predict the meteorite's fall. After observing a solar eclipse in 478 BCE, Anaxagoras had worked out that meteorites were actually heavy, rocky objects, held aloft by a centrifugal force. He warned that such rocks might one day fall to Earth, and when the Aegospotami meteorite crashed into the ground, he was proven right.

Diogenes likened the Aegospotami stone to fiery stony heavenly bodies similar to volcanic ejecta and posited that invisible stones travelled around along with the visible bodies of the heavens. Aristotle asserted that stones reported to have fallen from the sky were only terrestrial rocks that strong winds lifted and then let fall back to the Earth, denying the existence of solid bodies besides the Sun, Moon and planets. After the meteorite fell, it became a tourist attraction for the next 500 years.

To say that poetic licence was often applied to accounts of cometary activity is an understatement. A story tells how Methuselah's death was presaged by the appearance of a comet which coursed through the twelve signs of the zodiac. However, we know that no comet travels through the twelve signs of the zodiac.

According to sacred texts from India, the births of Krishna and of Buddha were foretold by moving lights in the heavens. Chinese records tell us of the appearance of a moving beacon in Heaven at the birth of Yu, the first ruler of the Celestial Empire, and again at the birth of the great Chinese prophet Lao-Tse. The ancient Greeks tell us that Aesculapius, the divine healer and first physician was born under a comet and Jewish tradition tells us that when Abraham was born a moving star was seen in the East.

Comets were believed to have accompanied the destruction of Sodom and Gomorrah, and another was believed to have appeared when Moses led Israel through the Red Sea and Pharaoh's host was swallowed up by the waves.

Some cultures read the message of a comet by its appearance. For example, the tail of the comet could look like the head of a woman with long flowing hair and therefore a symbol of mourning. Or it might appear to be a fiery sword, heralding war and death.

Two thousand years ago, the Roman astrologer Marcus Manilius summed up the prevailing opinion:

> Heaven in pity is sending upon Earth tokens of impending doom.[38]

Included in his list of cometary ills were blighted crops, plague, wars, insurrection, and even family feuds. Anything could be blamed on comets, and usually was. Bede the Venerable declared in the seventh century that:

> Comets portend revolutions of kingdoms, pestilence, war, winds, or heat.[39]

And the Roman writer Claudius gloomily stated that:

> a Comet was never seen in the Heavens without implying some dreadful event.[40]

The poet Virgil told of:

> the baleful glare of bloody Comets[41]

and of:

> dreadful Comets blazing in the sky[42]

The legends that developed around ancient sightings served to inspire dread in a comet's appearance. In the Babylonian *Epic of Gilgamesh*, a comet is associated with fire, brimstone and flood. The Mongolian Yakut called comets "the daughter of the devil" and associated them with destruction, storm and frost. Halley's Comet has been blamed for earthquakes, illnesses, red rain, and even the births of two-headed animals. Comets and disaster became so intertwined that in 1456, Pope Calixtus III excommunicated Halley's Comet as an instrument of the devil.

The Greeks and Romans viewed comets as a sign of bloody warfare and disaster and Cicero when writing of the civil war between Augustus and Antony said that "comets were the harbingers of the miseries that then befell them". The Roman historian Pliny (23 CE–79 CE) shared this view and it was his work that became the standard text on comets over the following centuries. Pliny recognised nine types of comets, each of which had a specific meaning based on their appearance.

In the second century CE, the Greek astronomer Ptolemy reported in his *Tetrabiblos* that comets contained everything you needed to make a detailed prognostication, provided you knew how to read the signs:

> They show, through the parts of the Zodiac in which their heads appear and through the directions in which their tails point, the regions upon which the misfortunes impend. Through the formations of their heads they indicate the kind of the event and the class upon which the misfortune will take effect; through the time which they last, the duration of the events; and through their position relative to the Sun likewise their beginning.[43]

The effects of comets were supposed to last for one eighth of their period – this would most likely have been their period of visibility – and to begin in earnest when the Sun or Mars transited their place of closest approach to the Sun. They often heralded the rise of an agent, perhaps a war leader, religious leader, reformer or great trader. The ancient Greeks based their significance on their colours and shapes.

Josephus tells how at the time of the destruction of Jerusalem in 69 CE, a sword-shaped comet hovered for months over the city. It was widely believed that the malicious influence of a comet was a manifestation of the anger of the gods. It was further believed that the shape of a comet had something to do with its purpose, for example, as Pliny tells us, if it resembles a flute, it will have an unfavourable influence on music.

> If it resembles a pair of flutes, it is a portent for the art of music; in the private parts of the constellations it portends immorality; in relation to certain fixed stars it portends men of genius and a revival of learning; in the head of the northern or the southern serpent [i.e. Draco and Serpens] it brings poisonings.[44]

Another tradition derives from Nechepso-Petosiris and is preserved in the work of Johannes Lydus (fifth century BCE).

Notwithstanding this, comets haven't always been associated with bad events in history. Chaeremon the Stoic saw them as a good omen in his book *Treatise on Comets* and Hephaistio of Thebes (born 380 CE) saw comets as positive omens if they were in Cancer, Scorpio or Pisces. And when Augustus Caesar began his reign in 44 BCE he pronounced a comet then in the sky an omen of promise to himself and his people and also declared that it conveyed his departed uncle, Julius Caesar, to a place among the demigods.

A Comet blazed for seven nights together, rising always about eleven o'clock, visible to all in Rome. It was taken by all to be the soul of Caesar, now received into Heaven; for which reason, accordingly, Caesar is represented in his statue with a star on his brow.[45]

In 79 CE, the Emperor Vespasian refused to be frightened by the appearance of a comet:

This hairy star does not concern me. It menaces rather the King of the Parthians, for he is hairy and I am bald.[46]

Which would have been more impressive had he not died shortly afterwards. Throughout the medieval period, it was believed that every pestilence, plague or wonderful event was connected with signs in the heavens, especially comets. For centuries, comets inspired dismay.

This comet was so horrible, so frightful, and it produced such great terror in the vulgar, that some died of fear and others fell sick. It appeared to be of excessive length, and was of the colour of blood. At the summit of it was seen the figure of a bent arm, holding in its hand a great sword, as if about to strike. At the end of the point were three stars. On both sides of the rays of this comet were seen a great number of axes, knives, blood-coloured swords, among which were a great number of hideous human faces, with beards and bristling hair.[47]

We've probably established that comets were a big deal. But what does all this have to do with the Via Combusta? It's simply that this area of the sky has long been renowned as where many brilliant temporary stars have appeared throughout history.

Perhaps the most famous of these was the supernova of 134 BCE, the first in astronomical annals, and the star that resulted in Hipparchus – according to Pliny – compiling his star catalogue. Hipparchus (146-126 BCE) invented trigonometry, and constructed a catalogue of 1080 stars. We now know that his was not in fact the first star catalogue, which had been produced at least two centuries earlier by the Chinese astronomers Shi Shen, Gan De and Wu Xian.

Hipparchus' catalogue not only gave the (celestial) latitude and longitude of each star, but divided them according to their brightness into six magnitudes. This list has undergone few alterations up to the present day, except for the addition of a number of southern constellations, and it remained, with slight alterations, the standard one for nearly sixteen centuries.

The Chinese *She Ke* confirmed 134 BCE appearance by its record of "the strange star" in June of that year in the sieu (lunar mansion) Fang. The Chinese kept careful astronomical records of visible comets and novae and used different terms to describe them. A tailed comet was called a "sui-hsing", meaning a broom star, the 'broom' referring to the tail of the comet. A comet without a tail is called a "po-hsing", and a nova is called a "k'o-hsing", meaning guest-star. (A clear distinction was not always made between novae and comets without a tail.)

Another "guest star", as the Chinese called them, had been seen in Scorpio in 393 BCE. This appeared in the bowl-shaped asterism named Wěi, formed by the tail of the modern constellation Scorpio. It reached an estimated apparent magnitude of −1 and was visible for about eight months before fading from sight. In 125 BCE, another new star was noted by the Chinese in June in the sieu Fang.

The most ancient supernova to be recorded by the Chinese appears on and oracle-bone inscription from the reign of the Shang king Wu Ting (ca. 1400 BCE).

On the seventh day of the month, a *chi-ssu* day,
a great new star appeared in company with
Antares.[48]

This was also recorded by the Babylonians:

A comet arose whose body was bright like the day,
while from its luminous body a tail extended, like
the sting of a scorpion.[49]

This comet is recorded to have been visible to the naked
eye for twenty-nine nights. According to accounts given, it
had ten tails and stretched far across the sky and was more
extraordinary than anything ever seen in the heavens before.
Because of its apparent size, the comet of 1486 BC probably
came very close to earth and, assuming that a fragment
of it broke off and reach Earth, it has been blamed for the
colder climate and the subsequent food shortages that some
archaeologists have suggested occurred at the time.

The Chinese are also known to have been the first to
record sightings of what we now know as Halley's Comet.
Their observations of this comet go back to at least 240 BCE.
Halley's Comet has probably been in its current orbit for
16,000 to 200,000 years and produces the annual Orionid
meteor shower, the peak of which occurs around 21 October.
In pre-classical times, Halley's comet was a brilliant object,
perhaps as much as 1,000 times brighter than Sirius.

In 12 BCE, Halley's comet was followed by Chinese
astrologers for 56 days (26 August - 20 October) as it
made its way through the constellations before ending its
journey in Scorpio.

Lately, reproaches in the form of solar eclipses
and meteors have been in the sky. These great
strange signs were repeated and yet those in
official positions remained silent; rarely has

there been loyal advice. Now a bushy star has been seen in Tung-chin. We are very dismayed. The ministers, grandees, doctors and advisors are each to think solemnly as to the meaning of these changes and compare them clearly with the Classical texts: nothing is to be concealed...[50]

This "sparkling star" was first detected in the morning sky in the "Tung-Ching", which is a group of stars in the constellation Gemini and was "treading on Wu-Chu-Hou", which is another group of stars in Gemini. Because of the coming close approach to Earth, the comet's motion increased during the following days. On 20 October it went out of sight in the constellation of Scorpius.

It has become clear that Halley's comet was the harbinger of disaster in the Norman invasion of England in 1066, portrayed in the Bayeux Tapestry. It appeared in April at Easter time in Capricorn and shone for forty nights, waxing and waning with the moon. William the Conqueror hailed it as an omen of destruction to Harold of England just before the Battle of Hastings.

Over the island of Britain was seen a star of a wonderful bigness, to the train of which hung a fiery sword not unlike a dragon's tail; and out of the dragon's mouth issued two vast rays, whereof one reached as far as France, and the other, divided into seven lesser rays, stretched away towards Ireland.[51]

William of Malmesbury notes in his twelfth century *Gesta regum Anglorum* that the monk Eilmer of Malmesbury, upon seeing the 1066 apparition, stated:

You've come, have you? ... You've come, you source of tears to many mothers, you evil. I hate you! It is long since I saw you; but as I see you now you are much more terrible, for I see you brandishing the downfall of my country. I hate you![52]

That Scorpio was home to blazing stars was further emphasised in 941 CE, when a comet moved from Scorpio to Libra.

...a little before dawn, a luminous vapour, in the form of a column, had made its appearance, and every succeeding night it arose half an hour earlier than on the preceding night. When it had attained its full development, it looked like a spear (or like a porcupine), with the two ends thin, but thick around the middle. It was a little curved, like a reaping-sickle, with its back towards the south and its edge towards the north. ...Astrologers have written that it portends evil to the chiefs of Arabia. Allah only knows if this be true![53]

If anyone was left in any doubt as to whether the area of the sky from the end of Libra to early Scorpio gave birth to new stars, that doubt would disappear in 1006 when an eighteen year old baker's son in Cairo, Ali Ibn Ridwan was one of many to see a new star.

Ibn Ridwan had just begun his education in medicine and was already an accomplished astrologer when on the evening of April 30 he noticed a new star in Scorpio. Ibn Ridwan interpreted it as a portent of ill fortune and later noted (without offering specifics) that "calamity and destruction" followed in that year.

By the time of his death in 1067 or 1068, Ibn Ridwan had written more than one hundred works. Later to be known to Western astrologers as Haly, he wrote a commentary on Ptolemy's *Tetrabiblos* and it's here that we find his account of the spectacle he had witnessed in his youth.

I will now describe a spectacle [supernova 1006] which I saw at the beginning of my studies. This spectacle appeared in the zodiacal sign Scorpio, in opposition to the Sun. The Sun on that day was 15 degrees in Taurus and the spectacle in the 15th degree of Scorpio. This spectacle was a large circular body, 2½ to 3 times as large as Venus. The sky was shining because of its light. The intensity of its light was a little more than a quarter of that of moonlight. It remained where it was and it moved daily with its zodiacal sign until the Sun was in sextile with it in Virgo, when it disappeared at once...

The positions of the planets at the beginning of its appearance were like this: the Sun and Moon met in the 15th degree of Taurus; Saturn was at 12° 11' in Leo; Jupiter was at 11° 21' in Gemini; Mars was 21° 19' in Scorpio; Venus was 12° 18' in Gemini; Mercury was 5° 11' in Taurus; and the Moon's node was 23° 28' in Sagittarius. The conjunction occurred in the 15th degree of Scorpio. The ascendant of the conjunction when the spectacle appeared over Fustat of Egypt was 4° 2' in Leo. Also the tenth house (which included most of) Taurus began at 26° 27' in Aries.

Because the zodiacal sign Scorpio is a bad omen for the Islamic religion, they bitterly fought each other in many wars and many of their great cities were destroyed. Also many incidents happened to the king of the two holy cities (Mecca and Medina). Drought, increase of prices and famine occurred, and countless thousands died by the sword as well as from famine and pestilence.[54]

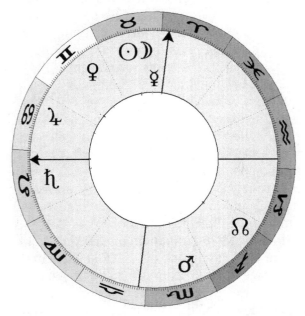

Ibn Ridwan's data were calculated rather than observed, as the Moon was in conjunction with the Sun at the time and therefore not visible. However, we can still calculate the the date of the sighting - 30 April. Other than the position of Mars, where there is clearly an error, the calculated positions are very accurate and give at time of approximately 11 am. However, the account states that the phenomena was in opposition to the Sun and therefore below the horizon. It seems that the it was not seen on the night of 29/30 April, but the following night and Ibn Ridwan calculated a chart for the previous day for astrological purposes.

Earlier interpretations of the text assumed that this phenomenon was a comet. However, it is clear that the body had a fixed position while the sun moved from Taurus to Virgo and was therefore a supernova. It was the brightest apparent magnitude stellar event in recorded history. This guest star was described by observers from China, Egypt, Iraq, Japan and Switzerland. Some sources state that the star was bright enough to cast shadows; it was certainly seen during daylight hours for some time and the modern-day astronomer Frank Winkler has said that "in the spring of 1006, people could probably have read manuscripts at midnight by its light." It appeared to be half the size of the Moon.[55]

There were two distinct phases in the early evolution of this supernova. There was first a three-month period at which it was at its brightest; after this period it diminished, then returned for a period of about eighteen months. Most astrologers interpreted the event as a portent of warfare and famine. It's possible that the star was erratically visible for up to ten years according to the Chinese Chronicle Sung Shih, which refers to a star visible in November 1006 through May 1016.

Traditionally, the astronomers of the Arab world were more interested in cyclic and predictable phenomena than those of an unexpected nature such as a "guest star". This would explain the low number of "guest stars", a term that has no equivalent in medieval Europe or in the Arab world.

Another supernova occurred less than half a century later – in 1054. This was another widely-observed event, with Arab, Chinese, and Japanese astronomers recording the star's appearance on 4 July 1054 CE. The explosion appeared in the constellation of Taurus (although in the zodiac sign of Gemini), where it produced the Crab Nebula remnant. At its peak, the luminosity of SN 1054 may have been four times as bright as Venus, and it remained visible in daylight for 23 days and was visible in the night sky for 653 days.

Rather than the Via Combusta referring to a single astronomical event that took place there, it appears to be related to a serious of phenomena, each of which served to further emphasise that there was an area of the sky that was dangerous and fiery.

6

GIVE IT TO THE GREEKS: THE STORY OF PHAETHON

O nce upon a time, back in the deep mists of time, it is said that the Sun used to travel along the path now marked by the Milky Way. And then:

The earth caught fire, starting with the highest parts. With all its moisture dried up, it split and cracked in gaping fissures. The meadows turned ashy grey; trees, leaves and all, were consumed in a general blaze, and the withered crops provided fuel for their own destruction. But these are trifles to complain of, compared with the rest. Great cities perished, their walls burned to the ground, and whole nations with all their different communities were reduced to ashes. The woods on the mountains were blazing, Athos was on fire...[56]

The Milky Way would now burn for evermore and the Sun had turned from its path to travel along the ecliptic, the path it still holds. All because the youthful Phaethon set the sky alight.

> There have been and will be many and diverse
> destructions of mankind,
> Of which the greatest are by fire and water,
> and lesser ones by countless other means.
> For in truth, the story that is told
> In your country as well as ours,
> How once upon a time
> Phaethon, Son of Helios,
> Yoked his Father's chariot,
> And because he was unable to drive it
> along the course taken by his father
> Burnt up all that was upon the Earth,
> And himself perished by a thunderbolt
> That story, as it is told,
> has the fashion of a legend.[57]

This story of celestial disaster in the far distant past is that of Phaethon (the shining). The most famous version appears in Ovid's *Metamorphoses* (8 CE), which is a Latin narrative poem in fifteen books that describes the history of the world from its creation to the deification of Julius Caesar. (The story appears much earlier in Aeschylus' lost play *Heliades* (fifth century BCE) and Euripides' *Phaethon* (lost play of about the fifth century BCE) as well as in other places.

Briefly, Phaethon's mother Clymene had boasted to him that his father was the Sun god Helios. Phaethon went to his father who swore that he would give Phaethon anything he asked for in order to prove his paternity. Phaethon wanted to drive his father's chariot (the Sun) for a day. Although Helios tried to talk him out of it, as the chariot was fiery hot and the horses breathed out flames, Phaethon was adamant.

When the day came, Helios anointed Phaethon's head with magic oil to keep the chariot from burning him. He instructed him on his route and Phaethon set off driving the horses Blaze, Dawn, Fire and Flame. He set the heavens on fire as he traversed the heavens, creating what is now called the Milky Way. Phaethon was soon unable to control the fierce horses that drew the chariot as they sensed a weaker hand. First Phaethon flew too high and encountered the celestial scorpion, its deadly sting raised to strike and he veered too high, so that the earth grew chill.

> His senses reel; he drops the reins aghast. And when the reins fall loose upon their backs, the horses swerve away and, unrestrained, gallop through tracts of air unknown and race headlong, out of control, running amok amid the stars fixed in the vault of heaven, hurtling the chariot where no road had run. And now they climb to highest heaven, now plunge sheer in breakneck descent down to the earth.[58]

The Sun moved wildly about the sky, finally to form the constellation Eridanus, which marked the path that Phaethon drove along – this was later also considered to be a path of souls.[59]

> The earth bursts into flame, the highest parts first, and splits into deep cracks, and its moisture is all dried up. The meadows are burned to white ashes, the trees are consumed green leaves and all, and the ripe grain furnishes fuel for its own destruction... great cities perish with their walls and vast conflagration reduces whole nations to ashes.[60]

Zeus was forced to intervene by striking the runaway chariot with a lightning bolt to stop it and Phaethon plunged into the Eridanos, the river that leads to the underworld.

His wounded body smoulders to this day and sends up clouds of steam. Even the light-winged birds that try to fly across the water fail to reach the other side and with a helpless flutter plunge into the heat.[61]

Helios, stricken with grief, refused to drive his chariot for days. Finally the gods persuaded him to not leave the world in darkness. Helios blamed Zeus for killing his son, but Zeus told him there was no other way. After his death Phaethon was placed amongst the stars as the constellation Auriga (the charioteer), just above the head of Orion.

In pity for the unceasing grief of Phaethon's sisters, Zeus turned them into poplars, from which, it was believed, their tears oozed forth and became amber, the stone of light.[62]

Both Ovid and Manilius told Phaethon's story as linked with the stars of Scorpio. Or more precisely, within the claws of Scorpio – that section of the sky where Libra meets Scorpio.

There is a region, where the Scorpion draws
The pincer pattern of his curving claws;
With curling tail, and jointed legs each side,
He spreads his limbs two constellations wide;
And sweating with black venom, does not fail
To threat the tortures of his twisted tail.[63]

The white streak of the Milky Way became known as the scorched path left behind by Phaethon's ride.

Many poets and historians give the story that Phaethon, the son of Helios, while yet a youth, persuaded his father to retire in his favour from his four-horse chariot for a single day; and when Helios yielded to the request Phaethon, as he drove the chariot, was unable to keep control of the reins, and the horses, making light of the youth, left their accustomed course; and first they turned aside to traverse the heavens, setting it afire and creating what is now called the Milky Way...[64]

Mighty cities burn with all their ramparts; realms and nations turn to ashes; mountains with their forests blaze...Then Phaethon saw the world on every side ablaze – heat more that he could bear.[65]

The story is similar to that of the Babylonian god Marduk, who in his earliest form was a solar deity. The story given on Akkadian cylinder-seals found in Mesopotamia describes how the peace of the solar system was disrupted by the arrival of the new god, Marduk, and traces the havoc among the planets step by step. If such an event took place in prehistory to be remembered by the Greeks and repeated in myth, it would be only logical to assume that other cultures did the same. And they did.

Tezcatlipoca, defeating Quetzalcoatl in ball-play (a game directly symbolic of the movements of the heavenly orbs), cast him out of the land into the east, where he encountered the sun and was burned.[66]

King Wan dreamt that he was clothed with the sun and moon...In the first month of spring, on the sixth day, the five planets had a conjunction in Fang...The conjunctions of the five planets in Fang brightens all within the four seas.[67]

The Chinese constellation Fang is roughly equivalent to Scorpio. That there was a genuine celestial event in this region of the sky is recorded in Aristotle's Meteorology:

> ...the stars...fell from heaven at the time of Phaethon's downfall.[68]

This comment has led to widespread speculation about precisely what phenomena the myth of Phaethon describes. Although some authorities argue in favour of a meteor, such a body would only be visible after it entered the atmosphere, seconds before it crashed whereas Phaeton's story implies that the phenomena was visible for some time. An active comet or a combination of the two would provide a much better source for the story. A comet appearing at sunrise would have a tail, shortened by perspective, pointing upward. It would then appear as if the Sun were chasing the comet as it apparently increased in size. Once Earth was within the tail of the comet, it's possible that the sky could glow with aurora and meteor showers. And although the common interpretation of the quotation below from the Biblical Book of Isaiah is usually believed to refer to Venus (or perhaps Jupiter), there is a school of thought that this describes such an event.

> How art thou fallen from heaven, O
> Lucifer, son of the morning.[69]

The Bible is also the source of what is to Westerners a highly familiar story of catastrophe resulting from astronomical phenomena. One that is believed to have originated from the same area of the sky – that of the Deluge.

7

A Long Time Ago

The idea that the Phaethon myth is a record of a real celestial event is not new. Plato, in his *Timeaus*, sees it as a record based on fact:

> But the truth of it lies
> In the occurrence of a shifting of the bodies in the heavens,
> Which move around the Earth,
> And a destruction of the things on the Earth by fierce fire,
> Which recurs at long intervals.[70]

And he notes that such events took place before recorded history:

> [w]hile, on the contrary, you and other nations commit only recent transactions to writing, and to other inventions which society has employed

for transmitting information to posterity; and so again, at stated periods of time, a certain celestial defluxion rushes on them like a disease; from whence those among you who survive are both destitute of literary acquisitions and the inspiration of the Muses. Hence it happens that you become juvenile again, and ignorant of the events which happened in ancient times, as well among us as in the regions which you inhabit.[71]

Some of the elements of the Phaethon myth can easily be associated with celestial phenomena. Cometary tails have been associated since antiquity with the manes of horses. The fear connected with such visions in the night sky remains in the modern word "nightmare". The Chinese constellation Fang – roughly equivalent to Scorpio – is said to be composed of four horses (four stars in the head of Scorpio) and is also called Tiansi, a celestial team of four horses.

Myths such as that of Athena being born fully formed from the head of Zeus are often interpreted as being descriptive of comet fragmentation. The effects of celestial phenomena are well recorded in myth and legend. For example, the Hindu account of Brahma and his followers describes how he notes the arrival in the sky of a small white body which, within an hour, grows to seem as big as an elephant before hitting the earth and causing a worldwide flood.

Such a large scale disaster suggests a supernova rather than a comet. A supernova is an exploding star that emits vast amounts of energy and was first proposed as a distinct class of objects in 1934 by the astronomers Fritz Zwicky and Walter Baade. What we now recognise as supernovae would have been described as comets in the past. (Although in Europe earliest known observation of what we now know to be a supernova was not until the 11th century CE, there were 90 probable novae and supernovae listed in Chinese records between 1400 BCE and 1700 CE.)

We know that explosions in the sky have profoundly affected the history of humanity. One example is that of the Antioch earthquake of 526 CE:

> ...those caught in the earth beneath the buildings were incinerated and sparks of fire appeared out of the air and burned everyone they struck like lightning. The surface of the earth boiled and foundations of buildings were struck by thunderbolts thrown up by the earthquakes and were burned to ashes by fire... It was a tremendous and incredible marvel with fire belching out rain, rain falling from tremendous furnaces, flames dissolving into showers... As a result, Antioch became desolate... In this terror up to 250,000 people perished.[72]

A celestial event on the scale as described in the Phaethon story would have had a major effect on the cultures in existence at that time. And around the end of the thirteenth century BCE the Bronze Age civilizations of the Aegean and eastern Mediterranean collapsed, for no clear reason.

Between 1206 and 1150 BCE, the Mycenaean kingdoms, the Hittite Empire in Anatolia and Syria and the Egyptian Empire in Syria and Canaan suffered interrupted trade routes and severely reduced literacy. In the first phase of this period, almost every city between Troy and Gaza was violently destroyed, and often left unoccupied thereafter.

Hattusas, the Hittite capital, was burned and abandoned, and never reoccupied. Areas were abandoned and the Hittite Empire went into obscurity for the next two centuries. Karaoğlan was burned and the corpses left unburied. Troy was destroyed at least twice, before being abandoned until Roman times. Up to 90% of small sites in the Peloponnese were abandoned, suggesting a major depopulation. Although cities like Athens continued to be occupied, they suffered from reduced trade and an impoverished culture, from which it took centuries to recover. For example, Aegean scripts used in Greece and Crete fell into oblivion. An entire written language was lost forever. There was a loss in crafts – lamps ceased to be manufactured and gold disappeared.

The decline in population can be seen by the decrease in the number of settlements in the twelfth century BC. In the fourteenth century, there were 320 settlements in Greece of which forty were densely populated. After the collapse, these settlements were reduced a hundred fold. For example, Messene and Triphylia had 150 known settlements in the thirteenth century BCE, but only fourteen survived into the twelfth Century BCE. Important sites were reduced to ashes by fire and others were totally abandoned.

In Mesopotamia, the cities of Norsuntepe, Emar and Carchemish were destroyed. After surviving for a while, the Egyptian Empire collapsed in the mid twelfth century BCE. The collapse has been seen as the worst disaster in ancient history, and cultural memories of the disaster survive in stories of a "lost golden age".

There are numerous theories that have been put forward to explain what happened. Some blame volcanic activity – the Hekla 3 eruption approximately coincides with this period. Earthquakes are another possibility. A swarm of earthquakes are believed to have taken place over fifty years sweeping areas from southern Italy to central Turkey.

Migrations and raids by tribes such as the mysterious Sea People have also been blamed along with a large rise in piracy, slave raiding and other attacks. This theory is backed up by the fact that the collapse coincides with the appearance in the region of many new ethnic groups. However, as the reasons for these migrations could be as various as drought, developments in warfare/weaponry, earthquakes or other natural disasters, the migration theory is not necessarily incompatible with other theories. One of which is that a supernova near Antares was the culprit.

Whole areas of Central Asia and the Near East were desolated and abandoned. Iranian tribes from the Northeast conquered most of Iran. Babylon was overwhelmed by an Elamite invasion.

And the effect spread still further. The north of Europe lost most of its dense population in the thirteenth century BCE. While tsunamis demolished Crete and Mycanae, as recounted by a number of writers including Homer, similar events stretched throughout Europe. Geologists' observations in a number of areas indicate that a huge wave overcame Europe. The West coast of Germany was flooded by an enormous wave that caused banks of silt to be created that today stretch twenty-five kilometres and up to ten metres high, even after more than three thousand years of weathering.

Even in India, the years 1250 to 950 BCE seem to be barren. Rangpur, the only remnant of the Harrappa civilisation, a fragment of the lost Indus Civilization, din't survive this period. The Shang, who lived along the Yellow River Basin in China, reached the end of their time being uprooted by the Chou, who would become the next rulers, sometime between 1122 and 1027 BCE.

And things weren't help by the climate change affecting the planet. Global cooling was especially evident from 1200 to 1190 BCE. In the Norwegian mountains, the snow line lowered by 400 metres. No glaciers were observed in the Eastern Alps until around 1200 BC when they reached far into valleys. Droughts occurred in north western Asia in 1150 and 1130 BCE and around the Black Sea. Neolithic sites in the Eurasian forest belt moved because of a drop in the water level of nearby lakes. Lake Naivasha in Kenya dried up. Heatwaves and droughts around 1250 BCE caused a recession of the water table worldwide and led to a much drier climate. After this, a warm, moist climate occurred before a global fall in temperature that would last until the mid-tenth century BCE.

Fire, famine and disorder had taken over the world. The chaos means that archaeological evidence of what happened is thin on the ground so it's hard to piece the story together.

The events that took place at this time are remembered in works by classical authors such as Hesiod in his *Theogony* (c.800 BCE) and the *Dionysiaka* of Nonnos (c.500 CE), which describe the battle between the gods involving a hot blast, hurricane winds, a darkened sun, blazing thunderbolts and the earth catching fire. Many elements of these stories, including flaming, winged serpents encircling the sky and crashing to earth go back much earlier than Hesiod and some can be seen in the second millennium BCE Babylonian conflict between Marduk and Tiamat. Variants of these myths occurred worldwide and persisted for millennia.

The Old Kingdom in Egypt had fallen into ruin. The Akkadian culture of Iraq, thought to be the world's first empire, collapsed. The settlements of ancient Israel were gone along with Mesopotamia. And at this time apocalyptic writings appeared that still fuel religious beliefs today.

It is possible that a comet, or the break-up of a large comet as some have postulated, was the culprit. Multiple impacts could have many effects leading to earthquakes, tsunamis, volcanic activity and subsequent climate change. Failing harvests and subsequent famine would lead to then massive migrations known to have taken place during this period. An idea of the scale of such a disaster can be seen through accounts of the Khatanga meteor from the Taurids that fell in Tunguska, Siberia in 1908. Over seven hundred square miles of dense Siberian forest were scorched and flattened.

In 1869, an Italian astronomer, Giuseppe Zezioli, noted eleven meteor falls between 1 and 7 November. The same year, the British astronomer Backhouse, observed five meteors falling on 6 of November and Tupman observed eight meteors falling over the Mediterranean Sea. All these meteors had come from the same area of the sky, the zodiac sign Taurus and so became known as the Taurids. Because of their occurrence in late October and early November they are also known as "Halloween fireballs".

Comet Encke, which accompanies the Taurids, was discovered in 1786 and is believed to be the remnant of a larger comet that broke apart thousands of years ago and formed the source of the Taurids. This stream of matter is the largest in the inner solar system and the Earth takes several weeks to pass through it, causing an extended period of meteor activity. The Taurids are also made up of weightier material than other such streams, being formed of pebbles instead of dust grains.

In 1950, the astronomers Whipple and Hamid discovered that the orbits of four Taurid meteors coincided with the orbit of Comet Encke as of 4,700 years ago and that, as of 1,500 years ago the orbits of three other Taurid meteors coincided with each other but not with the orbit of Comet Encke. They concluded that the latter three Taurids were formed by a breakup 1,500 years ago of a fragment that had in turn broken off from Comet Encke much earlier.

The Taurid meteor stream peaks around 30 June in daylight hours but is visible in the night skies of November. The Earth passes through each dense part of this belt of debris every 3,000 years.

A number of Chinese records of meteor observations over the last two thousand years are now known to be of the Taurids. The daylight June Taurids (the Beta Taurids) are active during 5 June to 18 July and the night time Taurids fall into two streams, the Northern (active from 12 October to 2 December 2 with maximum activity during 4-7 November) and Southern (active from 17 September to 27 November with maximum activity during 30 October to 7 November.

If Phaethon's event was that of a comet, we know that it appeared to come from the direction of Scorpio and if the Taurids are remnants of Phaethon's comet, it may be relevant to point out that they can be viewed at the time when the Sun is in the Via Combusta.

8

WET

Almost every culture tells stories of how once it rained a lot. It rained so much that life was almost wiped off the planet. This rain was accompanied by fires, earthquakes, debris falling from the sky, hurricanes and prolonged darkness and coldness. Sometimes, there was also a full solar eclipse. The world was never the same again.

The earliest account of the Deluge appears in the fragmentary Sumerian *Eridu Genesis*, which can be dated to the seventeenth century BCE. According to this, the gods had decided to destroy humanity – their reasons for doing so are obscure – and the god Enki warned Ziusudra (also known as Atrahasis) of what was due to happen, advising him to build a large boat. After a flood that lasted seven days, Ziudsura made appropriate sacrifices and prostrations to Anu (sky-god) and Enlil (chief of the gods) and was given eternal life and left to repopulate the earth.

The story is told again in the eleventh tablet of the Babylonian Gilgamesh epos. One of the quests that Gilgamesh undertook was to search for Ziusudra in order to find the elixir of eternal life. Travelling through many northern lands, Gilgamesh finally reached a mountainous land, guarded by scorpion men. (These gave entrance to Kurnugi, the land of darkness and opened the gates for the Sun god Shamash as he travelled out each day, and closed the doors after him when he returned to the underworld at night. The word girtablilu, Scorpion-Man, was a reference to the claws of Scorpio.) After they recognised his divine nature, Gilgamesh crossed this land and it was dark for many days before he reached his destination. Chilled by the north wind, he reached a great sea, "the waters of death", which he crossed and on the other side he found Ziusudra from whom he obtained the plant of eternal youth. However he never ate the plant, because it was stolen from him by a serpent on his trip home.

For most people in the West, the story is most familiar as the Biblical account of Noah's ark which appears in the Book of Genesis. (Two non-canonical books – the Enoch and Jubilees, both later than Genesis – elaborate on the story saying that God sent the flood to rid the earth of the *Nephilim*, the titanic children of the *Grigori* the "sons of God" mentioned in Genesis, and of human females.)

According to this version, God decided that because of the wickedness of humanity he would cause a flood to cover the earth. He commanded Noah to build an ark to save Noah's family, and animals and birds. Once Noah had built the ark, rain fell for forty days, the water rose for 150 days and the mountains were covered by water. The ark came to rest on the top of a mountain and the water receded for 150 days until it had gone. Noah opened the ark and sent out first a raven, and then a dove to see if the waters had receded. He left the ark with the animals God placed a rainbow in the sky as a sign that he would never again destroy the Earth by water.

The version of the story that appears in the Quran, written in the seventh century CE, is very similar except that only Noah and a few believers enter the ark.

If this flood was a genuine event, we would expect that stories about it would survive worldwide – which is what has happened.

According to the Norse Edda the hero who escapes the Deluge with his wife in a big vessel is named Bergelmer.

> The waters rose, the Earth became dark, the ocean serpents beat the water. The stony hills dashed together. Earth sank into the ocean. The bright stars fell from heaven. The fire rose up to heaven itself.[73]

The Mayans said that the sky approached the Earth and in one day all perished. In Persian mythology, the earth was full of malign creatures fashioned by the evil Ahriman. The angel Tistar (the star Sirius) descended three times, in the form of man, horse and bull respectively, causing ten days and nights of rain each time.

In the ancient Egyptian *Book of the Dead*, Thoth, the Moon god, described how the flood was God's way of punishing the disobedient and evil.

Those from the Lower Congo told a story of when the Sun once met the Moon and threw mud at it, making it dimmer, so causing a flood. According to the Greeks, Zeus was determined to destroy humanity with a deluge and promised the other gods that he would create a new race of perfect beings. However, Prometheus, the fire god warned Deucalion, who escaped together with his wife, Pyrrha in an ark, which after the tenth day came to rest on a mountain.

The Yazidi of the Sinjar mountains of northern Iraq believe that the Deluge occurred not once, but twice. Chinese legends tell how, in the reign of the Emperor Ya-hou, a bright star came from the Yin constellation, just before a great planetary upheaval. In ancient Peru, the hero who survived the flood did so by plotting the unusual movements of stars. An ancient Jewish tradition tells that the Deluge was caused by God changing the places of two stars in the Pleiades.

The ancient Hindu account of Brahma tells of him noting the arrival in the sky of a small white body which grew as big as an elephant before hitting the Earth and causing a worldwide flood. The Mahabharata relates how Manu built a ship to survive this deluge. As Manu was meditating by the banks of the Chirini, a small fish came to him and asked for protection. Manu took pity on this fish, placed him in an earthen vessel, and raised him. When the fish grew large, it asked Manu to put him in the Ganges and later to place him in the sea. At this point, it warned Manu that a flood was coming that would destroy the Earth. The fish commanded Manu to build an ark, taking with him the Seven Sages (to preserve the ancient knowledge), and seeds from all plants, so they could grow again when the flood subsided. (There is no mention of taking animals on board.) When the flood waters rose, the fish returned and guided the ship with an attached rope. After some years, the ship finally found solid land on the tallest peak of the Himalayas, to which Manu tied the vessel. The fish then revealed himself as Brahma.

In ancient Peru, it was said that once all the people were drowned by a great flood, except for six people, who were saved on a floating device. The hero who survived the flood by climbing a mountain did so by accurately plotting the unusual movements of stars.

Mexicans have the story of Coxcox, who together with his wife Xochiquetzal, escaped the cataclysm in huge boat after being forewarned and advised by a divine being. The Inuit of Alaska, the Luiseno of the Lower California, the Chickasaws, the Iroquois, the Sioux, the Akawais, the Zuni Indians, the Aztecs and many more all share same memories of the time when the Earth nearly died.

In the Ugrian version of the flood, the god of the sky Numi-Tarem, decided that he must destroy the devil Kulya-ter with a fiery flood. He built an iron ship for the gods and a covered raft for humans. Numir Tarem flew to heaven with his iron ship, while the people went through the fiery flood, where most of their ship was burned except the last of the seven layers of their covering.

Most of these accounts describe a torrential, long-duration rainstorm, sometime accompanied by a huge tsunami. The water is often described as hot, sometimes as burning rain. Supernatural creatures are often associated with the flood, typically giant snakes or water serpents, birds, horned snakes, a fallen angel, a star with fiery tail or a tongue of fire – their descriptions sounding remarkably like those of comets. In many cultures, it was believed a huge celestial body, which passed very close to Earth, caused the disaster.

There are numerous theories about what the flood stories represent and most authorities agree that there is no evidence of a single huge flood, which covered all the mountains of the world.

One hypothesis is that flood stories were inspired by ancient observations of fossils. Although the Greeks, Egyptians, Romans, and Chinese commented in ancient writings about seashells and/or impressions of fish that they found, it was Leonardo da Vinci who postulated that an immediate deluge could not have caused the layered and neatly ordered strata he found in the Italian Apennines. The Greeks believed that the earth had been covered by water several times and cited the seashells and fish fossils that they found on mountain tops as the evidence for this.

Some geologists believe that dramatic flooding of rivers in the distant past might have influenced the myths. One of the most recent, and controversial, hypotheses is the Ryan-Pitman Theory, which argues for a catastrophic deluge about 5600 BCE from the Mediterranean Sea into the Black Sea.

There has also been speculation that a large tsunami in the Mediterranean Sea caused by the Thera eruption (c. 1630–1600 BCE) was the basis for the myths. However, this tsunami hit the South Aegean Sea and Crete and did not affect cities in the mainland of Greece, therefore it had a local effect.

Another theory is that a meteor or comet crashed into the Indian Ocean in prehistoric times around 2800-3000 BCE and created the undersea Burckle Crater, generating a giant tsunami that flooded coastal lands.

Until the nineteenth century, the story of the flood was commonly accepted as a factual account of an event and taught as a worldwide catastrophe. Gradually, churches began to teach that the flood was a localised event, if indeed it happened at all. But those who were convinced that the flood was a true, historical event spent endless hours studying the Bible so that they could work out precisely when it did happen.

James Ussher (1580/1581 – 1655/1656) was Archbishop of Ireland and a Calvinist who prepared what he believed to be an accurate chronology of Biblical events. His most famous work was to determine that the date of creation was the nightfall preceding 23 of October 4004 BCE – as the Sun entered what we now know as Scorpio. (Ussher's original calculations gave 25 October based probably on using Kepler's *Rudolphine* Tables, 1627, which gave the equinox on Tuesday October 25, although modern calculations place it on Sunday October 23.)

Ussher's chronology first appeared in *The Annals of the Old Testament,* his book first published in London in 1650. A similar chronology was published by John Lightfoot in 1642–1644. He also deduced that creation began at nightfall near the autumnal equinox, but in the year 3929 BCE. Autumn, rather than spring, was thought to be more likely as it marked the beginning of the Jewish New Year. Ussher's proposed date of 4004 BCE wasn't very different to the estimates of the Venerable Bede (3952 BC). It was widely believed that the Earth's potential duration was six thousand years corresponding to the six days of creation. Martin Luther favoured 4000 BCE as a date for creation and Johannes Kepler concluded that 3992 BCE was the probable date. The Mayan calendar dates the creation to 11 or 13 August 3114 BCE. The scientific consensus is that the age of earth and our solar system is actually about 4.54 billion years.

Ussher supplied a variety of dates for Biblical events, including that of the flood which he told us authoritatively ended 5 May 1491 BCE on a Wednesday. This is obviously not the only date claimed for Noah's flood. Others include 2304 BCE, 3000 BCE, 2500–2300 BCE and 7 December 2349 BCE.

These dates are based on the fact that the Bible tells us that the flood began on the seventeenth day of the second month. One problem with Ussher's dating – obviously not the only one – is that we don't know whether this is the second month of the civil or religious calendar.

If the timing of the flood is counted according to the Jewish religious calendar, which began in the spring, it would have occurred sometime in mid to late May.

If we assume it's the civil year, the date refers to 17 Heshvan, the second month of the civil year that began at the autumn equinox. (Heshvan is the only month in the Jewish calendar that does not contain any festival.) The flood ended the following year on the 27th of Heshvan – at the end of October or the beginning of November. Most of those who supply a date agree on one in November.

John Pratt,[74] a member of the Church of Latter Day Saints, is categorical in stating that by using astronomy to calculate the start date of the flood, we end up with Saturday 16 November 2343 BC with the ark being loaded a week prior on Saturday 9 November 2343. Or he could have said when the Sun moves from 28 Libra to 5 Scorpio and the Moon ends up in Scorpio. (Pratt's dating includes offerings of Adam's first breath of life on Saturday 17 October 4070 BCE, the expulsion of Adam and Eve from the Garden on Sunday 9 April 4001 BCE and Enoch's birthdate on Friday 19 September 3378 BCE after 6 pm.)

Rosh Hashanah, the Jewish New Year, is celebrated in mid-September. The second month begins in mid-October with seventeen days being at the close of October. Although the modern Jewish New Year falls on a different day in September every year, the ancient Hebrew calendar appears to place 31 October as the date of the great flood.

The day that Noah boarded the ark and the flood came upon the earth to destroy the world is the day that cultures all over the world remember the dead. The day that we still celebrate as Halloween.

Whether or not there was a worldwide catastrophe as outlined in deluge myths is open to debate. What is clear is that in folk memory the stories are associated with celestial phenomena and with the constellation of Scorpio, or more accurately with the area of the sky we now define as the Via Combusta.

9

KNOCKING ON
HEAVEN'S DOOR

The Milky Way, which we see as a milky circular band, is one of the most distinctive features of the night sky. It appears as a bright ring of light in the sky, inclined at a steep angle to the celestial equator. There's a prominent area of gas clouds near the Galactic Centre known as the Dark Rift (because of the light being blocked) which appears to divide the band of light into two paths. The Dark Rift looks like a giant dark gash in the Milky Way and ends at the southern crossroads, the crossing point between the ecliptic and the Milky Way. When a planet (including the Sun or Moon) entered the Dark Rift, it could travel to the underworld and thence to heaven.

The brightest part of the Milky Way begins in Scorpio. It crosses the ecliptic as a giant arch across the sky on the borders between Taurus and Gemini, and on the other side of the ecliptic on the borders of Scorpio and Sagittarius. Stars and star groups in those areas were extremely significant for ancient people who regarded them as portals of energy and spirit and as doorways to heaven and the underworld.

The intersection of the circles between Taurus and Gemini is known as the silver gate of heaven. The intersection of these two circles between Scorpio and Sagittarius is known as the golden gate of heaven. The Galactic Centre lies visually from our solar system along a line that passes through the golden gate.

The crossroads of the ecliptic and Milky Way are not affected by precession, but some ancient beliefs stated that it was only possible to go to heaven on the two solstice days. This was because in order to take the right path, the constellations that serve as gates to the Milky Way must "stand" upon the "earth," or rise heliacally at the equinoxes or solstices.

The doctrine of two gates through which the soul ascends and descends is drawn from the neo-Pythagorean philosophers Numenius and Cronius. This region of the sky was formerly known as the Gate of Cancer and the southern stargate was known as the Gate of Capricorn. The placement of the gates here is attributed to Porphyry and Numenius (second century CE) when the solstices were in Capricorn and Cancer, but this dates back to an earlier time as the idea of solstices as gates were alluded to in Homer's Odyssey. Ovid saw the sign of Scorpio as one of the two gates to heaven, the other being the opposite constellation of Orion.

As the galactic plane precesses around the zodiac, its inclination to the equator changes. It was at around 3000-4000 BCE that the crossroads lined up with the equinoxes. Therefore, the gates of heaven are usually connected with two bright red stars near the Milky Way – Antares and Aldebaran. The constellations of Taurus and Scorpius marked the equinox approximately 5,500 and the solstice 15,000 years ago. As the souls travelled along the Milky Way, Antares lay in wait to receive them.

The Sumerian *Epic of Gilgamesh* contained the first reference to this gate. After the death of his companion Enkidu, Gilgamesh searched for answers about how to obtain eternal life from his ancestor Ziusudra (equivalent of the Biblical Noah) who lived in the centre of the heavens with the gods. After Gilgamesh crossed the celestial sea he came to the gate in the Mountain of the Sun guarded by scorpion men. This gate opened to a passage that led to a paradise in which there was another sea with a central island where Ziusudra dwelt.

The Mayans knew it as the "soul's road" – to be travelled after death and it was depicted by the Cosmic Monster, with his two heads symbolising the crossing points of the ecliptic. The crossing between Scorpio/Sagittarius was known as the black road and led to the underworld and the crossing between Taurus and Gemini was the white road that led to the upper world. The Mayans venerated the Milky Way as the World Tree and regarded the star clouds that form the Milky Way as where all life came from. During winter, it was called the "White Boned Serpent."

At the base of the World Tree lay a scorpion – commonly identified as sinaan, a constellation roughly equivalent to Scorpio. (Sinaan is a constellation that is visible until early November when it then disappears for about fifteen days.)

The Barasan of North-western Amazonia saw a polarity between the Pleiades and Scorpio, considering the Pleiades to be the serpent's tail and Scorpio to be the serpent's mouth. The Quiche Mayans referred to Scorpio as a doorway to the underworld and Pleiades as the snake's rattle.

Greek traditions regarding Hades place it around the southern crossroads of the Milky Way and the ecliptic.

In Honduras and Nicaragua the Sumo believed that their Mother Scorpion, who received the souls of the dead, lived at the end of the Milky Way. In North America the Pawnee and Cherokee said that the souls of the dead are received by a star at the northern end of the Milky Way where the path divides.

> He [God] directs the warriors on the dim and difficult path, and women and those who die of old age upon the brighter and easier path. The souls journey southwards; at the end of the celestial path they are received by the Spirit Star.[75]

The star mentioned is believed to have been Antares.

According to the Pythagoreans, at the centre of the universe burned a fire by which the planets and stars reflect light. Greek mystics believed that the spiritual nature of man descended into material existence from the Milky Way through one of the twelve gates of the great zodiacal band.[76] Men's spirits were thought to dwell in the Milky Way between incarnations.

In some cultures, the Milky Way was described as a stairway or ladder – such as Jacob's ladder. Others expressed it as a rope or tree (World Tree) leading into the skies.

The majority of Western nations imagined the Milky Way more as a "road" or "street" than as a serpent or than as a river. The Anglo Saxons called it *Watling Street* – the path of the Watlings, the giant sons of King Waetla. They also knew it as *Iringes Weg* or *Wec* and *Bil-Idun's Weg* - Iringe and Bil-Idun were descendants of the Waetla who were warders of the Bridge of Asgard, the Scandinavian heaven. In time the Asgard Bridge came to be given as a name to the Milky Way. It was also known as *Walshyngham Way*, the road where Mary went to heaven.[77]

The Welsh knew it as *Hynt St Ialm* (St James's Way) and *Heol y gwynt*, the way of the wind; the Italians as the *Holy Street to Loretto*; the Spaniards as the *Road to St Iago* (of Compostella), the Muslims as the *Hadji's Way* (to Mecca), the Romanians as *Trajan's Way*, after the Emperor.

The Vikings knew it as *Wuotanes Straza*, or "Woden's Street"; the Dutch called it *Vronelden Straat*, the "women's street ". The Finns knew it as *Linnunrata*, the "Birds' Way". An old Finnish and Estonian legend tells that once all the songs of all the birds of the world were turned into a cloud of white wings, representing winged spirits on their passage from earth to heaven.

Ancient Hindus knew it as the *Path of Ahriman*; the ancient Norse as the *Path of the Ghosts* going to Valhalla; the ancient Gaels as the *Hero-Way*, leading from Earth to Flatheanas, the land of eternal youth. Eskimos and the Bushmen of South Africa called it the *Ashen Path*, again the road for the ghosts of the dead.

The *Complaint of Scotland*, a Scottish work of 1549, speaks of the Milky Way as being called by mariners *Vatlant* (Watlin) streit and Gawin Douglas (1474-1522), in his Virgil's *Aenid*, terms the Milky Way *Watlingstete*. In medieval Germany it was known as *Jacob's Way*.

Chaucer, writing in the fourteenth century, says:

> Now, quod he thoo, cast up thine eye, See yonder, lo, he galoxie, Which men clepeth the milky weye, For hit is white; and some, parfaye callen hyt Watlyng strete.
> *Now he said, cast up your eye. See yonder, the galaxy which men call the Milky Way. For it is white and some, by my faith, call it Watling Street.*[78]

In its earthly form, Watling Street was one of the "royal roads". Part of the Law of Edward the Confessor, written in Latin around 1050, translates as "the peace of the King is of many kinds, one given under his hand. . . . Another, which the four roads enjoy, to wit, Watlingstrete, Fosse, Hikenildestrete, and Ermingstrete."

The laws of William the Conqueror reaffirm:

> ...on the three royal roads, that is Watelinestrete, Ermingstrete, and Fosse, whoever kills a man passing through the country, or makes assault on him, breaks the King's peace.[79]

A later Norman version of these laws reinstates the Ickneild Way:

> ...on the four roads, that is Watlinge stret, Erminge stete, Fosse, Hykenild, whoever on any of these four ways kills another who passing through the country, or assaults him, breaks the King's peace."[80]

In early Christian times the paths to major pilgrimage centres were known as the Milky Way and poets of the time saw these routes as reflections of the celestial pathways taken by the gods. Sometimes this was explained by the Milky Way being formed from the dust raised by travelling pilgrims.

With such religious associations being made, it should come as no surprise that Antares is associated with an archangel – Uriel – the Watcher of the West. Archangel Uriel, amongst other things, is the angel of repentance who holds the keys to hell in one hand and his famous fiery sword in the other. Uriel is also credited for warning Noah of the impending flood. Because of this close association with the Earth, Uriel acts as a channel between the Earth and the divine, bringing God's plan into the material world.

Accepted as an archangel by the Church for many centuries, Uriel was finally removed from the records in 745 CE as the Church became increasingly concerned with the prominence the public was placing upon angels. Until this demotion he was considered one of the most important angels. Saint Uriel was the most highly ranked angel to be treated this way.

Uriel the Archangel has never been a popular subject of artistic representation. A few images once graced churches in Rome, but Uriel fell out of favour with church officials in the early Renaissance period. Pope Clement III reportedly ordered the removal of Uriel's image from the church of Santa Maria del Angeli in Rome, and a painting in the church in Piazza Esedra was painted over. The reason seems to have been a mistaken notion that Saint Uriel the Archangel was somehow connected with the Johannine heresy which claimed that John the Baptist, not Jesus, was the true messiah.

The idea of heaven having two gates was known within Christians until the sixteenth century, when the idea of heaven being a physical place fell from favour. According to the Bible, Saint Peter was appointed gatekeeper of heaven by Jesus and in statues and pictures he generally shown as holding two keys.

The Milky Way was not only where souls travelled after death. In ancient belief when a soul incarnated, it came down from the higher heavens through the outermost sphere of the fixed stars and passed down through the planetary spheres, eventually entering a mother's womb on earth. Passing through the planetary spheres imbued it with a portion of each planet's nature. The theme of the planetary spheres appears in Romanian myth:

> Scorpia wanted to eat God's Mother [the Virgin Mary], but Saint George caught Scorpia and buried her at the seventh frontier and he said that when these frontiers fall then Scorpia will emerge to garnish the waters. [81]

The "seventh frontier" is the seventh crystalline sphere of Saturn, which lies just below the crystal sphere of the fixed stars. Traditionally (as immortalised in Dante's *Divine Comedy* – Paradiso XXI-XXII) the Virgin Mary resides in the final, tenth heaven.

Romanian folklore recognises a giant constellation *Sarpele*, which although often described as being equivalent to Serpens was much larger and also included Ophiuchus, therefore lying partly along the ecliptic and intruding on what we know as the zodiacal sign of Scorpio.

Sarpele was known as the *Road of Lost Men*, and in later folklore was the place where sinners stray when afraid of the Second Coming of Christ. This area of the sky leads away westwards from the brighter regions of the Milky Way and can be interpreted as a path of stars leading off into the darkness away from the Milky Way.

The Milky Way also bears a relationship to comets. Aristotle thought their appearance represented fire that originated from the Milky Way and that their vapours sank down to Earth and polluted the atmosphere, causing catastrophes. Comets would create a fiery road that led directly to hell. A number of different myths describe a large luminary other than the Sun journeying across the Milky Way. This idea appears in Phaethon's story and this body is considered by some to be a giant comet.

To find their final resting place, souls needed to travel along the road marked by the Milky Way, using the gates at either end. If they instead take a path brightened by a temporary light they could be led directly to hell. That is, if they took the path marked by the Via Combusta. Perhaps they should have remembered that milk is traditionally an antidote for the sting of the scorpion.

10

CLIMBING UPWARDS

According to the Bible, Jacob once had a rather strange dream:

And he dreamed, and behold a ladder set up on the earth, and the top of it reached to heaven: and behold the angels of God ascending and descending on it.[82]

That a ladder could take you to heaven was a common idea. In ancient Egypt, tiny ladders were placed in tombs to help dead kings make their way to heaven. Sometimes, an image of a staircase, rather than a ladder, would be used, or occasionally a rope, a rainbow, bridge, vine or cord. And often, travel to the upper world was by climbing the trunk of the great tree that stood at the world's centre.

There is an almost universal belief that in ancient – so ancient that it was ancient even to the ancients – times, heaven was much closer to Earth. It was so close that traffic between the two was common. But then there was a calamity that caused the ladder to collapse and the sky to be lifted to its current height.

In West Africa there are numerous traditions that tell of a time when the spirits in the sky mixed with earth bound humanity. The exchange is usually supposed to have been cut off by some human action. For example, the Fernando Po people say that the gods threw down the ladder after noticing a crippled boy ascending it, chased by his mother. Similarly, the Chinese believed that a ladder spanned heaven allowing regular exchanges.

Where did the ladder come from? The Tlingit of British Columbia told a tale of how the son of a great chief was once shooting arrows and decided to shoot a star next to the Moon. When the star darkened, he continued to shoot and none of the arrows returned to Earth. After a while he saw something hanging down very near him and, when he shot up another arrow, it stuck to it. He carried on and soon a chain of arrows reached him. Lying down under the arrow chain, he went to sleep. When he woke there was a long ladder reaching down to him from the sky. The ladder was necessary to allow the souls of the dead to reach heaven.

The Makka tells of a giant tree (that they likened to a ladder) that spanned heaven and earth. People would climb it until they reached the highest point of the tree, and then the sky. But the towering tree collapsed in a great fire. The Chamacoco tell of a time, before there was a Sun or stars, when an insect cut down the tree and it fell. The heavenly bodies were forced to move away from Earth. As the tree fell to the ground, a great flood came – it seemed to be the end of the world.

In ancient Babylon, the epic *Nergal and Ereshkigal* tells how Nergal (Mars) ascends a stairway to heaven to reach the assembly of the gods. He confronted the gods and for his pains he was said to have shrunk in size or become otherwise deformed.

The association of the destruction of the heavenly path

and Mars isn't peculiar to the Babylonians. The Makirtare of Venezuela have a story about a hero's ascent to heaven via a ladder formed from a chain of arrows. The builder of the stair was Mars – or a red star.

The Australian Jaralde tribe didn't know the use of bow and arrows. In their story, the hero Waijungari threw a lance to heaven which allowed him to climb to heaven, where he lived as the planet Mars. And ancient India's *Rig Veda*, tells how the divine champion Indra, the god of war and thunder) separates heaven from earth.

The Biblical account of the flood tells that a rainbow appeared as the flood ceased, showing the passage to heaven. In Hawaii, the story was that after the flood ended, Nu-u, who had survived in a great canoe, looked up at the Moon and thought it was the god Cane. This displeased Cane, and he came down on a rainbow to reprove Nu-u, realising it was a mistake, he left the rainbow behind him as a token of his forgiveness. It's generally assumed that the ladder is a representation of the Milky Way. That a red star – usually assumed to be Mars, but possibly Antares – is involved is repeated in numerous accounts from the ancient Near East, Australia and South America. Some people have chosen to interpret these stories literally – that there was once a luminous tree-like apparition that dominated the skies and that the solar system was substantially different to how it is today. There's lots of talk about plasma. Some people prefer to make life complicated.

There are commonly seven rungs to the ladder (sometime nine), the same numbers as the stars in the Pleiades, the location of the ancestors in Meso-America. The bolt of lightning, road of fire or dragon that came from above threw a stream of debris down to earth as the red planet descended. Again and again, the red planet, the god of war and thunder, is identified as the celestial body that ascends the ladder.

The concept of the Via Combusta may be even more ancient than we have so far considered.

11

I Found that Essence
rare

The idea of a path across the sky brings a different
picture to our minds than it would have done during
the height of astrology. For centuries, a complicated
system of varying amounts of spheres was believed to form
the heavens based on the cosmology of the ancient Greeks,
particularly that of Aristotle.

Centremost in this cosmology was the earth. The sublunary
sphere was comprised of the four elements (earth, water,
fire, and air). Next followed a series of concentric spheres,
firstly of the seven planets then the circle of the fixed stars
(including the signs of the zodiac). Outermost in this
scheme was the *Primum Mobile*, sometimes divided into
three spheres of the crystalline heaven, the first moveable,
and the empyrean, or highest heaven. In medieval thought,
the outermost was heaven created on the first day, the
firmament on the second day and made visible on the fourth
was the visible heaven where angels lived and were created.

This outermost sphere encompassed the universe as a whole and its turning initiates the motions of the inner spheres.

This obviously wasn't the only possible model of the universe. In the sixth century BCE, Anaximander had proposed a cosmology with the Earth shaped like a section of a pillar where the Sun, Moon, and planets were holes in invisible wheels surrounding it; through the holes, humans could see concealed fire. Eclipses came from the holes in the Sun-wheel's rim and that of the Moon being partially or wholly stopped up. Authorities disagreed over the number and precise qualities of each sphere, although seven, as Bede suggested, was commonly accepted. As time went on, the number rose to fifty and more.

The Sun and Moon were thought to move in and out of the firmament dome through a series of openings. The spheres form a compact whole in which there are no gaps, or an inner vacuum, and around which there is nothing.

The spheres are animate beings that are constituted of both matter and form. Each has a "soul" or internal moving force, which is set in motion by corresponding incorporeal substances – the separate intelligences that are associated with each sphere but distinct from it. These intelligences emanate from God – in some schools of thought they are angels. These intelligences were the reasons behind why unexplained things happened on Earth.

Everything under the sphere of the moon was subject to decay and change; above was immutable. Comets were closer to the Earth than the Moon since they could clearly not be in the unchanging sphere that contained the fixed stars. The ultimate source of motion is God, the Prime Mover, who "moves" the universe.

The cosmos was extremely ordered although the interconnected movements of the heavens were complex. Each successive sphere, moving outward from the centre, was physically closer to perfection. And each sphere moved in uniform, circular motion.

The furthest from the Primum Mobile was the earth, the place where man was expelled to from Eden. Living in the midst of decay and corruption, man inhabited a stationary world. The material world was itself a reminder of how short life was while the heavens offered eternity. Sin was a physical part of the universe. The four elements of the sublunary world – fire, earth, air, water were contrasted unfavourably with the immutable essence of the superlunary spheres.

The cosmos was divided not simply into regions of space as we see it today, but into areas that had both moral and physical qualities. These were not prey to "laws of nature", but had coherence from the act of benevolence that had created them. The divisions expressed ways in which God could express Himself. The spheres shared in His divine essence, but unequally, falling into a hierarchy, within which each was dependent upon that immediately superior to it.

Each body or substance had a place that was natural to it and a natural motion in relation to that place. Movement took place with reference to a fixed point, the centre of the Earth at the centre of the universe. There was a qualitative difference between the movements of a given body in one direction rather than in another in relation to that point. The natural behaviour of bodies depended, therefore, on their actual place within the universe as well as the substance of which they were composed. The sphere of the moon divided the universe into two sharply distinct regions, the terrestrial and the celestial.

The spheres were more powerful than anything in the sublunary sphere, with strong influences over the Earth and everything on it. And beyond the heavens lay the Empyreum, the purest and most powerful region of all, unsusceptible to change of any kind.

Aristotle's universe was at the basis of most intellectual ideas about cosmology after its reintroduction to the West through the Muslim world in the twelfth century, and it remained so until the scientific revolution of the seventeenth century. The spheres could only undergo only one kind of change: uniform motion in a circle, the kind of motion that could persist eternally in a finite universe. The idea that the motions of the heavenly bodies must be resolved into uniform circular motions dominated astronomy until the end of the sixteenth century.

One weakness of the systems postulating that the universe was made up of a series of concentric spheres was that they had to assume that the distance of each heavenly body from the earth was invariable. This made it impossible to account for some phenomena, such as variations in the apparent brightness of the planets and in the apparent diameter of the moon, and the fact that solar eclipses were sometimes total and sometimes annular.

Later Greek astronomers had tried to account for these facts by devising different systems, and the most important of these was that devised by Hipparchus in the second century BCE and later adopted by Ptolemy in the second century CE.

Ptolemy, in the Almagest, had adopted the view that his astronomical theory was merely a geometrical device by means of which to account for the observed phenomena, He supposed the planets moved in a circle about a point, not necessarily at the centre of the earth, but somewhere on a line joining the centre of the Earth with the Sun. In addition, he assumed that a planet moved in a circle about a centre, which itself moved in another circle, and so on, until a circle was reached of which the centre was stationary with respect to the earth, though not necessarily on it. The last, and innermost, circle was known as the deferent and the others as epicycles. To account for the precession of the equinoxes he postulated a ninth sphere.

The Ptolemaic system was recognised early in the thirteenth century as being the best geometrical device to account for observed phenomena and was favoured as the only system capable of serving as the basis of numerical tables.

In Aristotle's system, the spheres were formed of a very subtle ethereal substance, moving more softly than liquids and without any friction. It was free from change other than locomotion. The celestial spheres didn't consist of any material substance as we know it, but were zones of ethereal space.

The element that the spheres were composed of – aether, the fifth element or the quintessence – had no qualities (it was neither hot, cold, wet or dry), was incapable of change (with the exception of change of place), and by its nature moved in circles. According to Aristotle, the stars and planets were formed of the same substance.

Unlike the spheres, the earth was composed of four elements, earth, water, air and fire. Earthly bodies naturally moved in a straight line towards their natural place in the sphere of the element of which they were composed. In that place was the fulfilment of their nature and there they could be at rest. This was why to someone standing on the earth some substances (for example, fire, whose natural place was upwards) seemed light while others (for example, earth, whose natural place was downwards) seemed heavy. The tendency to move up or down depended on the nature of the substance of which a particular body was composed.

The four elements differed from each other only in their qualities (for example, earth was cold and dry while air was warm and moist). Changing one or both of its qualities transmuted one element into another. These transmutations were going on constantly, adding to the constant change in this sublunary region. The planets were judged to be small spherical regions of greater density or lucidity in the transparent ether.

The finer points of this system could – and have – fill volumes. However, for our purposes, we are simply concerned with how, and whether, a path of fire could breach the gap between two celestial spheres. Surely something so solid could not be breached by something as light as fire?

There are two things wrong with that statement. Firstly, it is of the nature of fire to rise upwards and secondly, the spheres weren't solid. It was common to refer to the spheres as so to indicate that they were real and too a material form. But they could not be seen – the term "crystalline" originally underlined their transparency. They didn't need to be solid to push the planets around. The hand of God did that. As time went on they began to be thought of as being made of a viscous jelly-like material. It was only much later when Ptolemy's system began to be widely adopted and a mechanical view of the universe accepted that they began to be thought of as solid or glassy.

Tenth century Islamic astronomers debated at length whether they were concrete, physical bodies or abstract circles. Ibn al-Haytham (Alhazen) was one of those to consider that the celestial spheres do not consist of solid matter as he outlined in his *Book of Optics*. Ibn Sina (Avicenna) was specific that heavenly substances differ fundamentally from earthly things and are made of aether. In the thirteenth century, the theologian Adud al-Din al-Iji maintained that the celestial spheres were "imaginary things" and "more tenuous than a spider's web".

The nature of the celestial spheres was a matter of concern for European scholars in the thirteenth century who were dealing with the implications of the rediscovered philosophy of Aristotle and astronomy of Ptolemy. In general, they believed them to be solid in the sense of three-dimensional or continuous, but not in the sense of hard. Consensus was that the celestial spheres were made of some kind of continuous fluid. By the early years of the seventeenth century, this was the most widespread view as it allowed a way of keeping the crystalline spheres in the wake of Tycho Brahe's proof that the comet of 1577 was above the moon and not below it as claimed by Aristotle and would therefore destroy the spheres on its flight if they were solid.

For a long time, comets and meteors had been believed to be

meteorological phenomena, not celestial. Aristotle contended that comets were not celestial objects, but were parts of the Earth that, when raised into the heavens, interacted with the element fire to produce the comets. Comets were vapours in the atmosphere of the Earth. To believe otherwise would make the idea of a perfect, changeless, unblemished heaven untenable. Once comets were seen to be part of the physical realm, the crystalline spheres had to be physical entities. Aristotle believed that the spheres must fill all space. But it appeared that comets followed a path that took them through the planetary spheres.

Anaximander's pupil Anaximenes, in the sixth century ,held that the stars, Sun, Moon and the planets are all made of fire. Plato had also considered that the heavens were made mostly from fire. Aristotle considered that there was a fiery region in the upper air that was dragged along underneath the circular motion of the lunar sphere. The Stoic view had it that the heavens were filled with *pneuma*, a combination of fire and air that became more pure with distance from Earth. Many medieval cosmologists supposed the heavens to consist of a fiery substance. For a gate to be opened to allow passage through the spheres, an earthly element would have to be allowed in – the obvious one being fire.

Although fire moves naturally upward in a straight line toward its natural place at the periphery of the universe, once it arrived it would either rest or move naturally in a circle. An ascent to heaven would have to be allowed by God. Most accounts of the medieval universe describe the spheres as if they were unbreachable. However, there is a traditional as old as that of the celestial spheres – that of the ladder that can be climbed through the universe.

These "flaming walls" as Lucretius[83] called the crystalline spheres carried the Sun, stars, and planets. Every mortal had to pass through these flaming walls to get to heaven. The soul ascending to heaven would travel along its fiery path until it reached heaven's gate.

12

FESTIVALS OF THE DEAD

The relationship between early November and a festival of the dead is very ancient. It's true that some cultures remember their dead at different times of the year. February was the month of choice for the Greeks and Romans and August for the Japanese and Chinese. A small number of cultures favoured May, but November is by far the most common.

The most well-known globally is the Mexican *Dia de Muertos*, which can be traced back to indigenous observances. The *Days of Death* celebrated in in the past around 17 November were among the most important Aztec festivals, and appear to have dated to Maya or even Olmec times, in the thirteenth century BCE.

The Aztecs had a variety of celebrations that honoured the dead, the most well-known those that took place in early August. However, there was also a festival dedicated to a god called Mixcoatl (identified with the Milky Way) that occurred at the start of November, during the month dedicated to him.

Dia de los ñatitas (day of the skulls) is a festival celebrated in La Paz, Bolivia, on 9 November. In pre-Columbian times, indigenous Andeans had a tradition of sharing a day with the bones of their ancestors on the third year after burial; however, only the skulls are used today. Traditionally, the skull of one or more family members is kept at home to watch over the family and protect them during the year.

Traditionally, celebrations of the dead are associated with the Deluge. The Aztecs' *Atemoztli* (Falling Waters) occurred every November 16, when the end of the Fourth Sun or Age, brought about by a world flood, was commemorated. The Mayas throughout Yucatan and Peten hung small packets of cake on the branches of the holy Ceibra tree. These sacrifices were intended for the spirits of the dead and the Ceibra tree was a living memorial of the Great Flood from which their ancestors survived by sailing to Yucatan.

In Hawaii, the annual *Makahiki* festival honours arrival of Lono at Kealakekua. He was a white-skinned, fair-haired god who recently escaped a catastrophic deluge and was associated with all manner of cataclysmic celestial events, together with devastating earthquakes and floods.

The ancient Persian New Year began after November 1, and was known as *Mordad*, a month sacred to the god of death. Mordad derived from the earlier Marduk of the Babylonians and was revered as the Lord of the Deep who caused the Great Flood.

Many ancient cultures at various times began their year at this time. For example New Year was celebrated by the Assyrians in the month *Arahsamna*, which is the equivalent to our October/November. In Egypt (according to Plutarch) the New Year began in the month *Athyr* (or Hathor) which was also equivalent to our October/November.

Some cultures mark the day simply in honour of the dead while others believe the dead come back to visit on this day. Lighting candles or lanterns is associated with this later custom in order for the dead to be able to find their way back.

In the Christianised world, the festivals of the dead – when the spirits of the departed welcomed back, when ghosts, witches and all manner of evils are abroad – evolved into the trappings of Hallowe'en. (Traditionally, Hallowe'en is also associated with the Deluge.)

Old Hallowe'en or Hallowe'en Old Style was celebrated on 31 October in the old calendar, at a time when the Sun was at 15 degrees Scorpio – at the end of the Via Combusta. This association is lost in modern times owing to the change in calendars.

England was particularly slow to adopt the Gregorian calendar, which was named for Pope Gregory XIII who introduced it by a papal bull on 24 February 1582. The new calendar was adopted later that year by a handful of Catholic countries with other countries adopting it over the following centuries.

A new calendar was needed because the previous Julian calendar assumes that the time between vernal equinoxes is 365.25 days, when it's actually eleven minutes shorter. The error accumulated until by the sixteenth century it was ten days and the spring equinox fell on 11 March. The calculation of Easter, the most important Christian festival, was tied to the spring equinox and removing those ten days would bring it back to the same relationship with the equinoxes the Julian calendar held when established in 325 CE. To stop the error happening again, a modified pattern of leap years was also introduced as well as a new method of calculating the date of Easter.

Protestant states initially ignored the new calendar and although England came close to adopting at an early stage, anti-Catholic feeling caused the idea to be dropped. It wasn't until 1752 that the demands of foreign trade and increased travel saw the eleven days from 3 to 13 September inclusive omitted from the English calendar.

When the decision was made in England to adopt the new calendar, it was only half reformed. The principle was that all events fixed to a particular date stayed on that date. However a second principle was that no property rights were to be affected and all financial transactions would run their full term. As the term "property" was defined widely in the eighteenth century, this applied to rents, wages and bills as well as grazing rights and inheritance on attaining the age of majority.

While social and legal activities moved forwards with the New Style, economic and agricultural activities stayed with the Old. There was no longer a common public calendar that encompassed religious, social, festive and agricultural activities – instead there were many calendars. Major towns and cities had their own civic calendars of public holidays, feasts, fasts, guilds, processions, elections, fairs and anniversaries. Although the religious calendar of the established church continued, less people adhered to it with the increase of dissenters and many feasts and saints' days were disowned by clergy.

Fairs were specifically exempted from the calendar reform. They were to change their nominal date to retain the same place in the season, effectively observing the Old Style. Not all did so. Festivals coinciding with certain saints' days and observances tended to go New Style as the church followed the new calendar.

One festival that did move was All Saint's or Hallows Day. It had originally been celebrated on the first Sunday after Pentecost (seven weeks after Easter Sunday) and from 607 CE on 13 May. In 835 CE the feast of All Saints was made an official holy day and moved to 1 November.

The vigil of All Saint's Eve – Hallowe'en – was observed as early as the feast itself. All Souls Day follows on 2 November and is a celebration of all those who have died and when the Roman Catholic Church prays for the faithful souls in purgatory. It came in a when a French Benedictine abbot, Odilo, from the monastery of Clugny initiated it in 998 CE. Odilo ordered that in all the monasteries over which he ruled a solemn mass should be celebrated on the second of November for all the dead who sleep in Christ. The example was followed by other religious houses, and it was gradually introduced elsewhere. In Christian iconography, Archangel Michael holds a pair of scales on the Day of Judgement which is recognised as All Soul's Day. In some areas of the country, celebrations continued into the night of 4 November, known as Mischief Night.

All Saints and All Souls Days were followed by Martinmas. From the late fourth century to the late Middle Ages much of Western Europe, began a period of fasting (that was later to be shortened and would be known as "advent" by the church) on the day after St. Martin's Day for forty days. The advent fast wasn't as severe as the Lenten one and abstinence was required only three days a week. Items to be excluded from the diet included meat, cheese and fat as well as wine, ale and honey-beer. The limited diet was occasionally supplemented by fish, often poached, from local rivers and streams. The faithful were also expected to abstain from love making, weddings, games and unnecessary travel.

St. Martin's Day celebrates the life of St Martin of Tours and is a feast time. Autumn wheat seeding was completed, and the annual slaughter of fattened cattle produced "Martinmas beef". At this time of year, hiring fairs were held where farm labourers would seek new posts. In many countries, including Germany, Martinmas celebrations traditionally begin at the eleventh minute of the eleventh hour of the eleventh day of the eleventh month, which meant that those who observed the Old calendar would celebrate Martinmas on 31 October. And Martinmas itself had always been associated with a celebration of the dead.

In Estonia, the age-old celebrations of souls visiting their former homes became associated with Martinmas.

At Martinmas, bonfires are built, and children carry lanterns in the streets singing songs for which they are rewarded with sweets. In pre-Christian Ireland, an animal was sacrificed on St. Martin's Eve and drops of its blood were sprinkled on the threshold, as well as in the four corners of the house to drive off any evil spirits and ensure prosperity for the coming year. Old Scottish and Irish folk beliefs declared that the ghosts of the dead returned to their old homes on Martinmas.

Martinmas was also treated as a sort of New Year – in areas of England, France and Germany, leases ended at Martinmas, rents were due, and servants left households in search of new employment. This association dates back centuries before – in his eighth-century chronicles, Bede (c. 672-735) noted that the Anglo-Saxon term for November was "blot monath" or "blood month," in reference to the slaughtering of animals that took place during that month.

One reason why these Christian festivals had originally fitted so neatly into the year was that they fell close to the Celtic festival of Samhain – the time of the coming of darkness and the forces of the dark, which was originally calculated to fall when the Sun reached 15 degrees of Scorpio. Samhain means "summer's end", according to the ancient two-fold division of the year, when summer ran from Beltane to Samhain and winter ran from Samhain to Beltane. (Samhain is still the name for the month of November in the Irish language.)

Bonfires played a large part in the festivities and people were said to have cast the bones of the slaughtered cattle on the flames (bonefires). Often two bonfires would be built side by side, and the people would walk between the fires as a ritual of purification. Sometimes, cattle and other livestock would be driven between the fires. This was the time of year that animals were brought in from the land. Meat, or winter food, was plentiful and bonfires, were used to burn any part of the animal which was considered to be unfit for eating. The bonfires also served the purpose of lighting the souls of the dead toward heaven.

In medieval Ireland, Samhain became the principal festival, celebrated at the royal court in Tara for three days. After being ritually started on the Hill of Tlachtga, a bonfire was set alight on the Hill of Tara to serve as a beacon, signalling to people all across Ireland to light their ritual bonfires.

The bonfire tradition was moved by the Puritans in the seventeenth century to the eve of Guy Fawkes Day in honour of the man who was convicted of plotting to kill the king and blow up the Houses of Parliament. An Act of Parliament designated each 5 November as a day of thanksgiving for "the joyful day of deliverance" and remained in force until 1859.

Although calendar changes add some confusion, it's clear that festivals of the dead have long been celebrated the world over at the point when the Sun is at the middle of Scorpio. Why at this particular time of year?

One clue lies in the association between festivals of the dead and the Deluge. Numerous cultures believe that seven celestial beings were saved from the waters of the flood. The Mexicans believe that the Deluge began when the Pleiades culminated and midnight and marked the start of the new year. Non-Biblical Jewish tradition relates that Noah regarded the appearance of the Pleiades at dawn as an omen signifying the onset of the flood.

And Australian aborigines, who held their own festival of the dead at this time of year, not only marked the start of their three day festivities by the culmination of the Pleiades, but also venerated those stars as the giver of rain.

Around 21 November each year, the Pleiades reach their highest point at exactly at midnight – the only time of year that they do so. At this time, the Pleiades is in opposition to the Sun. It rises in the east around sunset and sets in the west around sunrise, culminating when midway between rising and setting. Precession has caused the culmination of the Pleiades to occur later in the year than it did in the past – about a thousand years ago it would have coincided with a cross-quarter day (or Old Hallowe'en). Samhain took place (not only when the Sun was at mid-Scorpio, but also) when the Pleiades culminated at midnight – and as Antares rises. By mid to late November, Antares has disappeared from the night sky, while the Pleiades continue to shine. (Those cultures that celebrated festivals of the dead in May did so when the Pleiades rose just before sunrise. This happened in May two thousand years ago.)

The best time to see the Pleiades is at the new Moon as moonlight washes stars out of the sky. (When the full Moon occurs at the time of culmination it can occult the Pleiades and block them completely from view.)

The Pleiades and Antares offer gates to the underworld. A Moon in Scorpio at this time of year will be waning as it travels through the Via Combusta allowing maximum light to the Pleiades, allowing souls to easily enter – or leave – through the golden gate.

And every year, the world over, people remember their dead as the Sun leaves the Via Combusta.

13

THANK YOU FOR THE DAYS

The idea that the Moon's passage through the zodiac on certain days would have a malefic effect went hand in hand with the popular system of Egyptian Days. That they were ancient and well known amongst astrologers is attested to by the fact that Al Biruni includes a list of unlucky days in the Persian calendar in his *Chronology of Ancient Nations*. And that they remained part of mainstream astrology is shown by the fact that Tycho Brahe was credited with compiling a list of thirty-two unfavourable days – in Denmark they are popularly known as "Tycobrahs Days".

These days were called *dies Aegyptiaci*, because they were thought to have been pronounced unlucky by the astrologers of ancient Egypt. The justification for the term was sometimes that "Egypytian" was a term for "darkness". Some said they were days on which calamitous events had occurred in ancient Egypt, such as the plagues described in the Bible. It was argued that some plagues didn't make their way into Biblical accounts, which is why there was a higher number than ten.

Although it isn't clear from where they originate, the system of Egyptian Days does not correspond to the Egyptian system of lucky and unlucky days, which were much more prolific and varied from seven to fifteen days per month in one Egyptian calendar.

The Egyptian – or evil – Days provide the origin of the word dismal from the Latin *dies mali*. However, Chaucer (amongst others) took "dis-mal" to be derived from old French *dis mal*, i.e. "ten evils".

The Western tradition of the Egyptian days was thus well established before the medieval period, and may have been reinforced by Arabic calendars in which, from the ninth century onwards, had been incorporated ideas on such matters as the motion and influence of the stars, the mansions of the moon, and the predictability of the weather.

Unlucky days go back as far as ancient Chaldea and a reference to an "unlucky month" is to be found in a list of incantations contained in a document from the library of the royal palace at Nineveh. This was written in the Accadian dialect of the Turanian language, a language that was already obsolete by the seventh century BCE.

Ancient Assyria's unlucky days were originally associated with the lunar cycle. The beginning and the end of the month were particularly closely associated with divine decision making and lunar phases played an important part in omen astrology. Days were not simply bad or good –however, it depended on what you wanted to do with them. For example, both seers and medical experts were supposed to refrain from performing their arts on the 1st, 7th, 9th, 14th, 19th, 21st, 28th, 29th and 30th of the month of Nisan, whereas on the 17th only the medical expert had to refrain from business. However, it was unfortunate to seek a decision by divination on the 2nd, 4th, 6th and 10th of the month. Oddly, these days don't coincide with the seer's forbidden days. Certain hours of the days were better than others – for example, "at sunrise when the Moon is dim".

There are numerous references in ancient texts to favourable and unfavourable days. If anything of import was planned, a favourable day for the enterprise was selected. The phenomenon of lucky and unlucky days was also common in ancient Egypt and Rome where there existed elaborate lists indicating the days that were favourable

Hesiod in his *Works and Days* from the seventh century BCE distinguishes lucky days from others, and gives advice to farmers regarding favourable days. In an ancient calendar from 334 CE, twenty-six Egyptian days were designated.

The Romans traditionally believed that certain days were unsuitable for public business, because the gods would not accept the preliminary sacrifices required before battles or other actions of state.

From Anglo-Saxon times onwards, lists of unlucky days commonly appeared in texts. Some were ominous, others merely threatened misfortune, and still others were of mixed augury, partly good and partly evil. Saints Augustine, and Chrysostom denounced the use of unlucky days and the Church consistently forbade such practices – while ensuring that they days were noted in its calendars.

Three days in particular were thought of as evil – the first Monday in April (on which Cain was born) and August (when Sodom and Gomorrah were destroyed) and the last of December (Judas' birthday). Other lists gave six or twelve days. Bloodletting, eating goose meat and drinking were especially hazardous.

> Astronomers say that six days of the year are perilous of death; and therefore they forbid men to let blood on them, or take any drink; that is to say, January 3rd, July 1st, October 2nd, the

last of April, August 1st, the last day going out of December. These six days with great diligence ought to be kept, but namely [mainly?] the latter three, for all the veins are then full. For then, whether man or beast be knit in them within 7 days, or certainly within 14 days, he shall die. And if they take any drinks within 15 days, they shall die; and if they eat any goose in these 3 days, within 40 days they shall die; and if any child be born in these 3 latter days, they shall die a wicked death. Astronomers and astrologers say that in the beginning of March, the seventh night, or the fourteenth day, let the blood of the right arm; and in the beginning of April, the 11th day, of the left arm; and in the end of May, 3rd or 5th (lay, on whether arm thou wilt; and thus, of all the year, thou shalt orderly be kept from the fever, the falling gout, the sister gout, and loss of thy sight.[84]

These lists of days don't appear to be related to Egyptian days.

Bundled in with these lists would appear passages such as this taken from a Middle English Text on Planting and Grafting in Cambridge, Trinity College, O.5.26

Autumpnus, i.e. Heruest, bigynneþ atte firste degre of Libra and dureþ vnto þe laste degre of Sagittarii. þat partie of þe ȝere is colde & drie. In þat tyme regneþ melancolie and in þat sesone a man schal gadre boþe fruyt & corn. And also whan þat a man wole sowe his whete take hede þat þe sunne be from þe vii degre of Libra vnto þe xxix degre of Scorpio & principalich in Scorpio, while þat þe vii sterres beþ vnder erþe by day and aboue erþe by nyȝt.

*Autumn, i.e. harvest, begins at the first degree
of Libra and lasts unto the last degree of
Sagittarius. That part of the air is cold and dry.
In that time reign melancholy and in that season
a man shall guard both fruit and corn. And also
when that a man will sow his wheat take heed
that the sun be from the 7th degree of Libra
unto the 29th degree of Scorpio & principally
in Scorpio, while that the seven stars are both
under earth by day and above earth by night.*

When the Moon was in Scorpio, it was a bad time
for bloodletting. An English almanac of 1571 advises
specifically against the last half of Libra and the first half
of Scorpio.

No part of man's body ought to be touched with
the Chirurgicall instruments, or cauterie actuall
or potencial, when the Sunne or Moone, or the
Lord of the Ascendent, is in the same signe that
ruleth that part of man's body. Also Gemini, Leo,
the last halfe of Libra, and the first 12 degrees of
Scorpio: with Taurus, Virgo, and Capricorne, are
not good for the letting of bloud. Two days before
the change of the Moone, and a day after, is yll to
let bloud.
*No part of man's body ought to be touched with
the surgical instruments, or cautery actual or
potential, when the Sun or Moon, or the Lord of
the Ascendent, is in the same sign that rules that
part of man's body. Also Gemini, Leo, the last
half of Libra, and the first 12 degrees of Scorpio:
with Taurus, Virgo, and Capricorn, are not
good for the letting of bloud. Two days before
the change of the Moon, and a day after, is ill to
let blood.*[85]

Although unlucky days based on the calendar are the most commonly recognised, lunaria (prognostic books based on the lunar cycle) would offer short predictions based on the thirty days of the lunar month, apparently based on the lunar mansions although that had fallen away by the time the first Latin texts appeared in the ninth century. Sometimes, these would appear alongside the Egyptian days.

Egyptian Days first appear in a Western source in the calendar Fasti Philocaliani, dated 354 CE. They then disappear until the ninth century, when the genre appears in a variety of formats. (The commentaries of Augustine, Ambrose, and Marinus show that the Egyptian Days were known under this name in early times.) They first appear in Old English in the first quarter of the eleventh century CE. The oldest lists offered twenty-four days of the year that were unlucky. Over time, the number of days to be avoided increased. After the ninth and tenth centuries, texts on the twenty-four Egyptian Days are more frequently encountered. Although the term was occasionally used to describe other unlucky days, it is clear that it primarily meant the twenty-four day list.

There is occasional confusion about the precise dates. This is because they were originally expressed as a number of days counted from the beginning and end of the month. For example, January the days are 1st and 7th, that is January 1 and 7th from the end – or 25 January 25. This suggests that the original relationship was between the days and the lunar, rather than solar, month. The modern method of stating the date counting the days of each month consecutively from the first is found in the Egyptian, Jewish, and Chinese calendars, but ancient Greece counted the last ten days of the month backwards as did Rome. One custom known as the consuetudo Bononiensis (custom of Bologna) was to reckon the first 15 days (or in 31 day months the first 16) forwards and the remainder backwards – in other words, counting forward to the full Moon and backwards after that.

Some lists contained unlucky hours and in those only the indicated hours on the dates concerned were shown to be unlucky.

The most common list of days was:

1 and 25 January
4 and 26 February
1 and 28 March
10 and 20 April
3 and 25 May
10 and 16 June
13 and 22 July
1 and 30 August
3 and 21 September
3 and 22 October
5 and 28 November
7 and 22 December

It seems clear that the origin of the Egyptian Days lies with the lunar calendar, and it is for this reason that many commentators have associated them with lunar mansions. However, what is interesting from our point of view is that the Egyptian days of November are highlighted in one of the most common mnemonics to be seen in the fourteenth century.

Prima dies mensis et septima truncat ut ensis
Quarta subit mortem prosternit tercia fortem
Primus mandantem disrumpit quarta bibentem
denus et undenus est mortis vultie plenus
Tercius occidit et septimus ora relidit
Denus pallescit quindenus federa nescit
Terdenus mactat iulii denus labefactat
Prima necat fortem prosternit secunda cohortem
Tercia septembris et denus fert mala membris
Tercius et denus est sicut mors alicuius

Scorpius est quintus et tercius est nece cinctus
septimus exanguis virosus denus ut anguis
*The first day of the month and the seventh cuts
like a sword*

*The fourth leads to death, the third overthrows
the strong man*

*The first disrupts he who orders (or sends), the
fourth he who drinks*

*The tenth and eleventh are full of the face of
death*

*The third kills and the seventh strikes the coasts
(or the earth)*

*The tenth turns one pale, the fifteenth is ignorant
of treaties, alliances*

*The thirteenth of July immolates, the tenth
shakes to ruin*

*The first kills the strong man, the second
overthrows a company*

*The third of September and the tenth bring evil
to limbs*

*The third and the tenth are as the death of
someone*

*The fifth is Scorpius and the third is girt with
slaughter*

*The seventh deprives the manly of blood, the
tenth is as a serpent.*[86]

Only the Egyptian days of November are associated with
a Zodiac sign. And that sign is Scorpio – and the dates are
when the Sun is in the middle of Scorpio.

14

OUR HOUSE

God is the One Who made the sun a shining
glory and the moon a light and for her ordained
mansions, so that you might know the number
of years and the reckoning (of the time). God
created this in truth. He explains the signs in
detail for people who know. [87]

The system of lucky and unlucky days is believed to be
associated with the lunar mansions – although the
discussion of which came first can be of a chicken
and egg nature.

Simply put, the lunar mansions are the constellations
which the Moon moves through along the celestial equator
in its cycle around the earth and are a method for dividing
up the celestial sphere. Most consist of pairs of stars or
small groups of closely spaced stars and each begins with a
reference star as its starting point.

There are three main systems correlating to the lunar

mansions. They are called *nakshastras* in the Hindu/Vedic astrology system, *sieu* (xiu) in the Chinese system and *manzils* (mansions) in the Arabic system. Each mansion begins with a reference star as its starting point. There are differences between the various systems, but they tend to agree as to their component stars.

Although lunar mansions are clearly ancient, there is no consensus as to when they were first used or who used them first. The origin of the system was the topic of hot debate in the nineteenth century, particularly regarding whether they first appeared in India or China.

Some authorities consider the concept of the lunar mansions to be Babylonian in origin and that they were adopted into India later, from the literature found in the *Mul Apin*. Although in some form or other they were very ancient in India, they do not seem to have been fully recognised there until the seventh or eighth century BCE. The lunar zodiac was used in China in the twenty-third century BCE. However, recent research[88] shows that the formal model of twenty-eight lunar mansions appears to have been borrowed from India.

Pre-Islamic anwa, or asterisms, were used primarily for weather prediction and it is generally believed that when the pre-Islamic Arabs received the system of 28 lunar mansions from India, each lunar mansion was identified with one of the anwa.

Before contact with Greek based astronomy, pre-Islamic Arabs used a number of fixed stars and asterisms. After the introduction of Islam, a substantial amount of poetry, proverbs, legends and folk science was written down in Arabic texts and attention was paid to the star lore of the pre-Islamic and early Islamic Bedouins and farmers of the Arabian Peninsula. In the Books of the Anwa (Kutub al-anwā') that appeared from the ninth century onwards more than 300 old Arabic names for stars and asterisms have been recovered.

The *anwa'* dealt with potential times of rain linked with the risings and settings of certain stars. They defined the seasons and acted as markers for timing agricultural activities. The term *anwa'* has the sense of rain, hence the anwa' stars were associated with the rain periods. The singular term *naw'* (plural anwa') is defined as the dawn setting of a star or asterism in the west at the same time as an opposite star or asterism rises with the sun in the east. This tradition ultimately influenced the naming of individual stars in Western constellations.

Knowledge of the Indian lunar zodiac may have existed in the Arabian Peninsula in the late fourth or early fifth century prior to the birth of Muhammad. The system of "lunar mansions" is mentioned in some old Arabian poems that are pre-Koranic; and are also mentioned twice in the Koran (seventh century CE.) In the post-Muhammad period, during the Arab expansion, Arab scholars began to assimilate the sciences in Iran and India.

The lunar mansions were particularly significant in Arabic astrology and it is through the Arabs that Hellenistic astrology was transmitted to Europe during the Middle Ages. During the ninth to the thirteenth centuries CE, there were many writers in Arabic on astrology, and almost all include some treatment of the lunar mansions, usually derived ultimately from the Hellenistic system of Dorotheos of Sidon (first century CE) and was influenced by the Indian nakshatras.

The lunar mansions were not used by the Arab-Islamic astronomers in their astronomical work, but were restricted to astrology. References to the mansions are also to be found in Coptic and Persian texts. The Egyptians had a similar process, called "working stars" possibly derived from the Babylonians, based on the stars heliacal rising at ten day intervals.

Because of the link with the fixed stars, which change their positions with respect to the Sun's equinoxes with precession, there has been a tendency to either treat the mansions as sidereal than tropical, or to shift the mansion which is regarded as the first one in accordance with the shift of the vernal equinox.

The mansions' names often tie them to a constellation or sign of the zodiac, meaning that if the Mansions remain tied to the stars rather than the signs, then anomalies appear. For example, *Al Batn al Hut,* "the belly of the fish", from the constellation of Pisces will now be found in the tropical sign of Aries. Most of the texts we have today derive from Arabic writers of the tenth and eleventh centuries, which were sometimes printed centuries later with no updating.

What is clear is that the mansions are of great antiquity and that all of the systems are broadly similar. Their great age can be seen from the fact that the list began with the Pleiades, when those stars marked the vernal equinox, which would have been around 2300 BCE, although this was changed about the beginning of our era to stars in Aries.

Traditionally, in both the Indian and Arabic systems, the first mansion was *Al Thurayya* (Many Little Ones; Indian, *Krittika*) located in the shoulder of the constellation of Taurus. With the establishing of the Sun's position at the vernal equinox as the First Point of Aries and the start of the Zodiac, the mansion associated with the star Sheratan, *Al Sharatain*, became the first mansion. Sheratan (Beta Arietis) is one of the horns of Aries and it is also called *Alnath* – "the one that butts".

If the boundaries of the mansions are tied to a starting point in the tropical zodiac, which is usually 0° Aries, adaptations tend to be in discrete shifts, displacing the sequence through the whole span of a mansion or even two. If the system is taken as purely sidereal, then it cannot be fixed to any particular point and will shift gradually every year.

In the West, we are mainly familiar with a system of twenty-eight mansions, disseminated in Europe through

Islamic texts. Owing to precession as discussed above, this means that we have a variety of different positions given over the centuries to choose from.

However, except for when answering horary questions, Hindu mansions number twenty-seven.

The first complete enumeration of all the nakshatras seems to be given by the *Taittirīya-Samhitā* (seventh century BCE or earlier). Each of the mansions were the "wives of the Moon" in the Sanskrit. Twenty-seven wives with whom the Moon could not play favourites and with whom he was forced to divide his time equally.

Each nakshatra represents a division of the ecliptic similar to the zodiac (13°20' each). The starting point for the nakshatras is the point on the ecliptic directly opposite to the star Spica. This star is given as the exception in the Via Combusta, a place where its malefic effects don't apply.

(A twenty-eighth mansion involving the last quarter of the twenty first (i.e. *Uttarashadha*) nakshatra and the beginning of the twenty-second (*Sharavana*), is sometimes considered as a separate nakshatra by the name *Abhijit*.)

The sixteenth mansion, *Vishakha*, lies at 20 degrees of Libra to 3 20 of Scorpio.

Vishakha represents fiery lightning and is symbolised by a gate. This mansion is represented by not one god, but two, Indra, the king of the Gods, and Agni, the God of Fire. It equates to Al-zubana (Alcibene, Al Jubana) said by Al Biruni to consist of two brilliant stars, known by some as the "pincers" and they stand in a place "where the claws of Scorpio might be".

Al Biruni travelled to India in 1017 and became the most important interpreter of Indian science to the Islamic world, being given the title al-Ustdadh ("The Master") for his remarkable description of early 11th-century India. He wrote an encyclopaedic work on India called *Tarikh Al-Hind* in which he explored nearly every aspect of Indian life. This included discussions of astronomy.

It is this which has led our astronomers and the authors of *anwa* books astray; for they say that the Hindus have twenty-eight lunar stations, but that they leave out one which is always covered by the rays of the sun. Perhaps they may have heard that the Hindus call that station in which the moon is, the burning one; that station which it has just left, the left one after the embrace; and that station in which she will enter next, the smoking one. Some of our Muslim authors have maintained that the Hindus leave out the station Al-zuband, and account for it by declaring that the moon's path is burning in the end of Libra and the beginning of Scorpio.

All this is derived from one and the same source, viz. their opinion that the Hindus have twenty-eight stations, and that under certain circumstances they drop one. Whilst just the very opposite is the case; they have twenty-seven stations, and under certain circumstances add one.[89]

The oldest form of the lunar mansions recognises the Via Combusta.

15

HANDY

et's suppose you were a nineteenth century astrologer and wanted to know what the Via Combusta was. You might be a little confused if you were to read George Crabb's dictionary of 1851 to be told that the Via Combusta is, in palmistry:

...the line of Saturn when parted...[90]

This wasn't an anomaly. An 1895 theosophical book on Indian palmistry also mentions the Via Combusta as a line.

Name. Via Combusta. Location. Extends through hollow of hand to mount of middle finger.[91]

It often appears marked on Russian palmistry diagrams, although it seems to have disappeared from most Western palmistry texts. In one, it's clearly marked as representing a "dead individual". No doubt you'd like to know a little more, so from the aforementioned 1895 book:

> The line of Fortune or Saturn begins at the wrist lines, extends through the hollow of the hand to the mount of the middle finger. If this line be cut or severed it is called the Via Combusta; when this line assumes a double line in the middle of the palm it is said that you do more good to others than yourself.[92]

The Via Combusta had been included in palmistry texts from when they began to be printed. By the eighteenth century, it was familiar to palmists as an area of the hand that portended doom.

> I WAS, once, in some kind of Danger to have been drawn into a Plot; but my SNUBSY found it out, in the Palm of my Hand; and in Presence of a Minister of State, who, I can assure You, made no small Use of Her, convinc'd me, beyond Dispute, that I should bid fair for being hang'd, by Virtue of a crooked Line, that cross'd my Via Combusta. This frighted me from my foolish Purpose: But, I remember, I was strangely comforted, to discover, at the same Time, upon the Minister's opening his Hand too, That his Lordship had a Combusta, as dangerously mark'd, as mine was.[93]

No, I don't know who "SNUBSY" was either. Clearly, he was someone who was worth knowing though.

Not everyone was enthused about the inclusion of this line. For one, it didn't appear in everyone's hands and it was usually listed as being of lesser importance than the other, better known, lines. Jerome Cardan in his book *De Varietate* (On a Variety of Things) in 1559 offered a diagram of the hand consistent with other contemporary handbooks. While mentioning the main lines of the hand that are still familiar to palmists today, he mentions a line called the Via Combusta as being of little import.

The inclusion of the Via Combusta in palmistry texts highlights the strong association between palmistry and astrology. Johannes Rothmann was one of the first to emphasise these interconnections. His *Chiromantia Theorica Practica* was first published in 1595 and translated into English by George Wharton in 1652 to become the first book published on chiromancy in England.

Rothmann postulated that the mounts of the hand are ruled by the planets, and characters and signs will appear in the mount of the hand corresponding to their most dignified planet. This means that from looking at the hand it should be possible to describe the horoscope and vice versa. In his book, Rothmann gave several examples of the correlations between the natal chart and the hand, supported by sketches.

At the time, this was a whole new approach to chiromancy. However, Rothmann didn't apply astrological symbolism extensively to all the lines of the hand, and he persists in using the same interpretations for the main lines and the markings that had remained standard for centuries.

Over the next hundred and fifty years, chiromancy was to become steadily more astrological in nature.

While William Lilly was the central figure in the seventeenth century astrological world, it was Richard Saunders (1613-1692) who was the central figure in the study of chiromancy. Saunders produced his *Physiognomie, Chiromancie, Metoposcopie* in 1653 with an introduction and approbation written by Lilly who praises Saunders as the greatest chiromancer of the day. In 1671 he produced a second, enlarged, edition and in 1663 he published a more popularised version under the title of *Palmistry, the Secrets thereof Disclosed*. A further treatise on palmistry thought to be written by Saunders can be found as a short chapter included in *The English Fortune Teller* published around 1680.

Saunders' book was almost an exact copy of the work of the French palmist, Jean Belot. Jean Belot's first book on chiromancy was published at Paris in 1619 entitled I*nstruction Familiere et tres facile pour apprendre les sciences de chiromance et physiognomie.* It was reprinted in the text entitled *Les Oeuvres* de Jean Belot, first published at Rouen in 1640.

There is a strong astrological emphasis to Belot's work – for example, the signs of the zodiac are associated with each of the twelve phalanges of the fingers. Belot insisted that in order to understand chiromancy it was essential to understand the meaning and significances of the planets and the astrological signs.

Saunders used a translation of *Les Oeuvres*, although he does make one innovation in giving planetary rulers to the main lines of the hand. He quoted the Via Combusta as being a line of "an inferior degree"[94] that was also known as the "Milky Way".

By this time the area of the sky we know as the Via Combusta was so established that incorporating it into systems of divination related to astrology was inevitable. A palmist with little knowledge of astrology would know it meant something bad, and if the premise that the hand reflected the natal chart was correct, it should be found there somewhere.

16

STARGATE

A survey on remote viewing took place in California from 1977 to 1995, called "Stargate". It was funded by the CIA and was one of several projects established by the US Federal Government to investigate the reality, and potential military and domestic applications, of psychic phenomena.

The US had become aware of psychic research being conducted in other countries, but there was little reliable information available. Therefore, it was decided that the CIA and military intelligence should launch their own investigations.

Remote viewing attempts to sense unknown information about places or events. It was attempted with the results being kept secret from the "viewer" so that any incorrect results would not damage the viewer's confidence. The Stargate Project aimed to make the research of clairvoyance and out-of-body experiences more scientific. Originally there were at least twenty-two active remote viewers providing data. When the project closed there were only three. The project was finally closed because of inconclusive results:

> Even though a statistically significant effect has been observed in the laboratory, it remains unclear whether the existence of a paranormal phenomenon, remote viewing, has been demonstrated. The laboratory studies do not provide evidence regarding the origins or nature of the phenomenon, assuming it exists, nor do they address an important methodological issue of inter-judge reliability.[95]

The book *Remote Viewing Secrets* was written by Joseph McMoneagle, one of the remote viewers. Near the end of the book, he mentions an analytic study done to see if there were any time of day that were better than others for remote viewing. They examined the 1015 or so trials that were done at SRI.

It became apparent that the accuracy of readings spiked in accuracy 4 fold within an hour of 13:30 local sidereal time than any other time of day, and it plummeted at 18:00. (Another low point was at 6 hr LST.)

At a given LST and location – the same degree of the zodiac will always be ascending AND the same degree of the zodiac will be at the MC.

Press reports in 1997 pointed out that at 13.30 local sidereal time Virgo is on the midheaven. In fact, for Western astrologers 24 degrees of Libra is on the midheaven. The best results were found when the ascendant lay between 18 Libra and 10 Scorpio.

LST period	Quality results	Ascendant	Period of Asc.
13:30 +- 1h	Best	29 Libra	18 Libra - 10 Scorpio

The time when the Via Combusta is rising on the horizon corresponds to a time when individuals can best receive images of places in another part of the planet.

The period of worst reception was when the Galactic Center was rising at 26 Sagittarius – six hours later. Although it was known that radio noise from the galactic center interfered with reception of data from satellites and theorised there may be some connection, there was no real explanation for this pattern.

	LST	ASC	MC	DSC	IC
Galactic centre rising	18:25	26 ♐	24 ♎	26 ♊	24 ♈
Galactic centre on midheaven	22:40	23 ♓	26 ♐	23 ♍	26 ♊
Galactic centre on descendant	02:56	26 ♊	28 ♒	26 ♐	28 ♌
Galactic centre on IC	02:56	27 ♍	26 ♊	27 ♓	26 ♐

This is also the time period when the Via Combusta is crossing the MC each day.

Geoff Dean and Ivan Kelly's comments on this phenomenon in the *Journal of Consciousness Studies* state that we should expect to find this effect within astrological tradition if it's real "as a rule to work only when that area of the sky is ahead". They further stated there was no hint of it in astrological textbooks, citing *Christian Astrology*. Perhaps they were looking in the wrong place.

17

BUT WHAT DOES IT MEAN?

In general, interpretations of the Via Combusta by modern astrologers tend to be of the "Oooh, that looks bad," or "I usually ignore that because I'm not sure what to do with it," type.

In most astrologers' minds, it applies to horary astrology alone, and as we all know how strange astrologers who practice *that* type of astrology are, it isn't worth giving much attention to.

In the past, the Via Combusta has been taken into account when considering revolutions, mundane and event charts. And it's so obvious that it's bad, that many texts pay it only cursory attention. The focus is certainly on the Moon being located in that area of the chart, although from time to time texts make mention of significators in a horary question, or other planets in mundane charts or revolutions, being placed there. That being positioned in Scorpio alone is enough to make a planet worrisome is an idea familiar to

astrologers. Even non-astrologers through the centuries –
and even now in some quarters – are aware of this.

For example, a number of dates on the Islamic calendar
are strongly associated with early events of Islamic history
(for example, the day of Muhammed's death) and as such
days are commemorated as days of mourning, they are
avoided for marriage (and sometimes other ceremonies.
And Islamic calendars have one particular astrological
configuration marked on them – the dates when the
Moon passes through the sign of Scorpio. These three to
four days per month are known as "Qamar Dar Aqrab"
(the word "qamar" implies that the Moon actually has to
be visible – not simply known to be in Scorpio) and can
be found on any Shia Islamic calendar – (Sunni Muslims
don't observe this).

> Do not arrange for the wedding night to coincide
> with the moon going through the scorpion phase,
> for would not lead to a happy marriage.[96]

Some Shia Mulsims will avoid any activity if possible
when the Moon is in Scorpio – at least any activity of
import. Qamar dar Aqrab is classed as an unblessed period
and is seen as bad luck for marriage in particular, but also
for other major celebrations. In Pakistan, at the start of
the Moon entering Scorpio, it's traditional to give sadqa (a
charitable gift) of milk to help prevent the negative effects of
this lunar phase from harming the individual and his family.

Similarly, should you be tempted to take up phlebotomy
as a hobby, it would be wise to take the advice offered in
texts such as this fourteenth century manuscript:

> Autumpnus, i.e. Heruest, bigynneþ atte firste
> degre of Libra and dureþ vnto þe laste degre of
> Sagittarii. þat partie of þe ȝere is colde & drie.
> In þat tyme regneþ melancolie and in þat sesone

118

a man schal gadre boþe fruyt & corn. And also whan þat a man wole sowe his whete take hede þat þe sunne be from þe vii degre of Libra vnto þe xxix degre of Scorpio & principalich in Scorpio...

Autumn, i.e. harvest, begins at the first degree of Libra and lasts unto the last degree of Sagittarius. That part of the air is cold & dry. In that time reigns melancholy and in that season a man shall guard both fruit & corn. And also when that a man will sow his wheat take heed that the Sun be from the 7th degree of Libra unto the 29th degree of Scorpio & principally in Scorpio...[97]

When the Moon was in Scorpio, it was a bad time for bloodletting. To be more specific, when the Moon was in the Via Combusta, you would be well advised not to let blood. An English almanac of 1571 advises specifically against bloodletting during the last half of Libra and the first half of Scorpio:

... Gemini, Leo, the last halfe of Libra, and the first 12 degrees of Scorpio ... are not good for the letting of bloud.[98]

As far back as Anglo-Saxon times, texts gloomily told how ignoring such advice could have dire consequences:

Ða ealdan læ ces gesetton on ledonbocum þæt on æ lcum monðe beoð æ fre twegen dagas þa syndon swiðe d'e´ rigendlice æ nigne drenc to drincanne. oþþe blod to læ tenne forþam þe an tid is on æ lcum þara daga gif man æ nige æ ddran geopenað on þara tide þæt hit bið (his) lifleast. oððe langsum sar. þæ s cunnede sum læ ce 7 let his horse blod on þæ re tide. 7 hit læ g sona dead...

The doctors of old wrote in Latin books that

there are always two days in each month on which it is very hurtful to drink any (medicinal) potion or to let blood, because there is a time on each of these days that if one opens a vein on this time, it will cause death or protracted pain. A doctor knew this and bled his horse on such a time, and it lay dead immediately.[99]

There are plenty of astrological texts from the sixteenth century onwards that offer definitions of the Via Combusta and advice on how to interpret it. And a persistent lack of clarity appears in these texts.

Also if the Moon be in via combusta, the matter is dubious and difficult to be Judged:[100]

...it is dubious to give Judgment.[101]

The lord of the ascendant in the via combusta, the question is corrupted.[102]

Astrologers who are slightly more definite in their approach write their analyses as if they were shaking their heads sadly while doing so. Words such as "unfortunate", "unsafe" and "weakening" occur again and again.

... unfortunate, and weakening to any planet that happens to be in it.[103]

If you find the Moon in Via Combusta ... it is not safe for the artist to pass judgement.[104]

In both beware of the beginning of Scorpio, and the end of Libra, for such is the Combust Way, and portends no good in such matters, nor in few others indeed.[105]

As far back as the first century BCE, Dorotheus had described the Moon in the Via Combusta as "corrupted" and "ineffectual", quoting both Babylonian and Egyptian sources. Hundreds of years later, Nicholas Culpeper took the same vaguely disapproving approach.

> ... portends no good in such matters, nor in few other matters.[106]

This is why by the time we reach the seventeenth century, at the height of the art of horary astrology, astrologers recast such interpretations as advice against judging a chart in the first place. After all, there was a good chance that it was the fault of the querent in any event.

> If the Ascendant falls in the Via Combusta the querent may have second motives.[107]

But what did astrologers actually do with it? Given that William Lilly is seen as the horary astrologer in the eyes of many, it's probably worth taking a moment to see how the great man approached the Via Combusta. In *Christian Astrology,* Lilly delineated a few horaries with the Moon in the Via Combusta. In the chart on page 415, where the Moon is at 8 Scorpio 20, Lilly answers a question about which of the husband or wife would die first. Lilly states that there were many serious reasons why the question was asked and uses the Moon to show the wife's conditions, which are commensurate with those of the Moon – she died soon after the question was put. However, he doesn't directly reference the Via Combusta.

Another example occurs on page 468, where the Moon is at 6 Scorpio 20; this was a question related to bewitchment. In this situation, the querent was very ill and the Moon was taken to indicate the fear felt by the invalid of being attacked by witchcraft. Again, the Via

Combusta isn't directly referenced. On Page 231, in the chart "If Presbytery Shall Stand?", Lilly notes that the Moon at 13.37 Libra is as entering the Via Combusta, but only lists it as a testimony for his judgement. Lilly's chart examples provide little evidence that he took account of this condition, much less that it prevented his judging the chart. Perhaps it was simply too obvious – and in any event, in the charts cited there were plenty of other factors that answered the question without Lilly having to devote brain power to analysing it.

Although everyone agrees that the Via Combusta is A Bad Place, astrological authorities are a little more circumspect when it comes to defining what form that badness takes and how bad it actually is. On the one hand, William Lilly says that it's one of the worst debilities for the Moon and on the other John Gadbury excludes it from his table of dignities and debilities. Johannes Schoener also doesn't refer to its score in his tables, although he does relate the work of Antonius de Montulmo who states that Via Combusta is a -2 (a surprisingly conservative score considering all the negative comments that are made about this position by other authors). Perhaps because while astrologers such as Lilly, Al Biruni and Bonattus suggested that judgement should be deferred when the Moon is in the via combusta, many of them considered deep down that you could get away with it so long as you were careful.

> When the Moon voyd of Course, or in Via Combusta, the Combust way; All Matters or businesses propounded, go unluckily on: therefore the Astrologer ought to understand the Matter propounded perfectly, or else he will give but poor content to the Querent therein.[108]

If you insisted on pinning an astrologer down and threatened to beat them around the head with a big stick unless they told you precisely how to interpret it, chances are they'd make mutterings along the lines of, "It's a bit like an eclipse innit?"

> A birth Moon in that arc was considered to be as afflicted as if it was in an eclipse condition...[109]

> ... it is reckoned next to an Eclipse.[110]

> It is ... said to be as strongly adversely (sic) as a lunar eclipse.[111]

> ... the Moon who suffers there as much as during an eclipse.[112]

With modern astrologers being less familiar with interpreting eclipses, the "I'm not sure what it is, but it sounds worrisome so I'll blame Uranus," approach has become popular. Barbara Watters suggests that we should treat the Via Combusta in the same way as a Moon/Mars conjunction, while the Indian astrologer Abhishekh Sharma is of the view that it is more akin to a Mars/Uranus conjunction.

Ignoring the tendency to dump things on Uranus when we're not sure what to do about them, and the premise that it's vaguely dodgy, we find that one place the Via Combusta is referenced in pre-seventeenth century texts is in relation to bloodletting. There were numerous positions the Moon could hold believed to be detrimental to making the cut to draw blood. Libra and Scorpio in general are often cited as signs to avoid.

> ... it being forbidden to make incisions when the moon is in Scorpio, Libra or Sagittarius.[113]

> Also ... the last halfe of Libra, and the first 12 degrees of Scorpio ... are not good for the letting of bloud.[114]

Concerning the time of the Moneth these generall cautions are to be obserued, that he be not let bloud in any member with chirurgicall instrument:
The Moone being in ... via combusta ... [115]

More commonly however, and especially in explicitly astrological texts, the interpretation of the Moon in the Via Combusta is generically "bad". "Bad" can mean a whole range of things. Some more pessimistic astrologers have gloomily pointed out that, in their opinion at least, it couldn't get any worse.

Likewise if the moone be in the via combusta ... it threatneth death.[116]

The Lord of the ascendant ... in the way called Via Combusta, sheweth death.[117]

Let not the Moon be ... in the combust way; for that signifies an ill end.[118]

... it is evil and a sign of death or of long sickness &c.[119]

If you're fortunate enough to hold onto a thread of life, it's probably wise to decrease any risk by staying firmly put.

When the Moon shall be in the combust way ... in the beginning of a journey, the person will either fall sick in his journey, or shall be otherwise grievously troubled and molested.[120]

The threat might not be directly to the querent however. In certain circumstances, attention is drawn to the vehicle itself. Although few of us need to check the time to launch ship nowadays, John Gadbury's detailed sailing rules can easily be applied to a plane take-off, or, more dully, turning the key in the ignition to drive to work.

> When in the figure ... you may then be bold to pronounce great Danger and misfortune to attend such ship or vessel that is so launched, or that under such a position either weigheth anchor or sets sail.[121]

In fact, the preceding comment suggests that even parking might be a worrying activity at such times.

Money was as much a worry to astrologers of the past as it is to those of today. William Ramesey takes pains in Astrology Restored (primarily a comprehensive guide to electional astrology – he thought that horary was A Bad Thing) that is almost completely culled from the works of Ibn Sahl and Haly, to point out that the Moon in the Via Combusta should be avoided for financial transactions, especially when it comes to loans.

> And Haly saith, If the Moon be in Via Combusta ... it signifieth no good to the Lender; but to the Borrower...[122]

Ramesey would never have had the temerity to contradict authorities such as Haly. However, it took a lot to convince Ramesey of anything, and he was aware that not everyone agreed with such an interpretation. His continued analysis is one of the most petulant statements he makes in his book.

> This is Halies opinion; you have but just now heard it is neither good for the Borrower or Lender at such a time; you may follow which you please, and in your curiosity try them both, and follow which you finde most true; a little experience will soon clear the doubt: however it is no ways good to lend any thing in the hour of Saturn.[123]

It might be helpful to remember that this is the man who told the story of a dinner guest swooning at the sight of a custard and thought leeks were evil. Ramesey expended a lot of his energy in worrying about getting things precisely right. Perhaps he was right to worry. In more general terms, the Via Combusta can hint at damage to the sight, perhaps even blindness. This is similar to interpretations given to comets, or the conjunction of the Moon with various fixed stars and constellations (such as with the Pleiades).

> The Moon in *via Combusta*, and the Sun in *via Lactea*, denotes great danger to the Eyes; and if the unfortunate Planets shall be in the Horoscope or opposite thereunto, it presageth blindness.[124]

It's probably obvious that no-one with any sense would elect a marriage chart with the Moon in the Via Combusta. But just in case you are foolish enough to attempt such a thing, Simmonite hammers the point home when discussing electing charts for weddings.

> Let not the Moon be ... in the combust way, for that signifies an ill end.[125]

Those astrologers who didn't predict doom and gloom in a generalised form appear to have chosen their favourite negative interpretation. However, some authorities preferred a more comprehensive approach, bringing together all of the possibilities discussed above. Ramesey was one of those to develop a comprehensive approach.

> ... this is the worst Impedition the Moon can have, especially in Marriages, and in all matters belonging to women, also in selling, buying, and in travelling or going a journey.[126]

Given that the Moon is a natural ruler of the feminine, it should come as no surprise to find that the Via Combusta is much worse for women.

> Seventhly ... when she is in the *via Combusta* ... this, saith he (referring to Haly), is the worst of all Impediments, especially in Marriages, and all matters of Women, in buying and selling, and in Journeys.[127]

Once in a while, attention is paid to other planets falling in the Via Combusta – most notably in revolutions – although it seems that at least some astrologers applied it to nativities.

> Venus, ruler of the year in via combusta: humiliations occasioned by women.[128]

> Mercury, ruler of the year, in via combusta anxieties, tribulations, adversity, losses in business.[129]

> (Mercury) If this planet be found in the combust way ... and at the same time slow in motion, it declares a trifling superficial character, perpetually engaged in unworthy objects, stunning us with impertinent remarks, with useless niceties, or with unapt disquisitions.[130]

Given that many of the older texts quoted above aren't easily accessible books – or at least have not become so until recent years – the only interpretations available to many astrologers during the twentieth century have tended to be of the "that's not very nice – avoid it" sort. That has led to modern astrologers developing their own interpretations – either through studying piles of charts, or, more flamboyantly simply making a good "guess".

> I call it the earthquake zone.[131]

> If the Ascendant falls in the Via Combusta the querent may have second motives.[132]

> Jonathan Clark ... has found that the Via Combust Moon often indicates the distress of the querent.[133]

> For example, I took my driving test with the Moon in the Via Combusta, and I had an accident on the way to the test centre.[134]

> One bank found that by scheduling loan committee meetings when the Moon was neither void of course nor in the via combusta produced an immediate increase in the number of collectable loans. Those workers hired when the Moon is in the via combusta are often found to have more than just exaggerated their abilities.[135]

Barbara Watters apparently failed in her quest to ignore it (although it's hard not to wonder if she really tried very hard considering how many things she associated it with in the end) and decided that events took sudden, contradictory, unpredictable and contrary turn with the Moon there. She connected it to war, violence, accidents, disasters, the sudden deaths of persons controlling the question and the destruction of property asked about.

Sue Ward's analysis of charts is equally gloomy. She has pointed out that the Moon in the Via Combusta often occurs in charts that deal with illness, death, fear and issues like imprisonment matters.

Marc Edmund Jones left no stone unturned in his analysis in his book *Horary Astrology*.

> The practical meaning of the Moon in the via combusta is an unsettled state of affairs that resists judgment and that involves a perverse self-satisfaction in the confusion. If the question or the problem can be seen, by the regression of perspective, to be an attempt to put such a chaotic condition to advantage, or to make some use of a baffling realignment in the general situation at a time when the lines of specific influence seem to be beyond identification, it is possible to proceed. Such questions would concern the subtle loss of morale in an organization, or the state of a person who, while completely dissatisfied with the existing circumstances in his life, is yet entirely devoid of any idea of what he wants, or what he would like to do. Also there are the cases where something akin to this momentary or even persisting disintegration will exist behind the scenes and will be verified on investigation, but where the querent is entirely unaware of its existence.[136]

While Jones effectively reduced its meaning back to the "slightly dodgy" arena, those who choose in modern times to spend their leisure time casting spells and invoking beings who might prefer to be left alone with a nice cup of tea are a little more definite about the negative outcomes that can be expected by anyone foolish enough to engage in such activities while the Moon is in the Via Combusta.

Magick begun in this period can result in immediate loss. Losses and destructive results can also be delayed thus surprising you later with some unexpected reversal. This is similarly seen with the Void of Course period. However, the effects typically have a far greater impact during the Via Combusta.

> Spells for prosperity or wealth are most likely to seek destructive means to carry out their mission. For example, a spell for wealth is most likely to result in injury or death as a means to acquiring money. Even though this may not be the magician's intent, unless great care is taken, nature will seek this level as the path of least resistance during this destructive period.[137]

It's always possible that you could be faced with some of the people Ebenezer Sibly had come into contact with who had Mercury in the Via Combusta.

> Mercury ... in via combusta shews the native not to be wise, but rather stupid, and dull of understanding, impertinent, troublesome, a dissembler, and very silly creature...[138]

However, if it's permitted to have a favourite interpretation (perhaps, better, a favourite expression of an interpretation), I personally would hand all my votes to that of Richard Thomson's – a man who clearly was worn to a frazzle by some of his clients.

> ...yet the Moon appearing in the Via Combusta, is evidence of some degree of deceit, which I perceive to be in thee; thy disguise, and assumed voice...[139]

THE END

1.　　Al Biruni, R. Ramsay Wright (Trans.) *The Book of Instruction in the Elements of the Art of Astrology.* Kessinger: USA, 2010.

2.　　Edward Phillips, *The New World of English Words.* London, 1658.

3.　　Elisha Coles, *An English Dictionary Explaining the Difficult Terms that are Used.* London, 1677.

4.　　Nicholas Gyer, *The English Phlebotomy.* London, 1592.

5.　　Joseph Blagrave, *The Astrological Practice of Physick.* London, 1671.

6.　　Joseph Moxon , *Mathematicks Made Easy.* London, 1679.

7.　　Nathan Bailey, *An Universal Etymological English Dictionary.* London, 1737.

8.　　Abu Mashar (tr. Charles Burnett) *Abreviation of the Introduction to Astrology,* ARHAT, US p.35.

9.　　Alcabitius *Introduction to Astrology* by Al-Qabisi or Alcabitius, (translated Burnett, Yamamoto and Yamo) Warburg Institute: London, 2004.

10.　　WJ Simmonite, *The Key to Scientific Astrology.* John Story: London, 1896.

11.　　Francis Barrett, *The Magus.* London, 1801.

12.　　Digitale Bibliotheek voor de Nederlandse Letteren, Die 100 capittelen van astronomijen, accessed December 2011, <http://www.dbnl.org/tekst/huiz006capi01_01/huiz006capi01_01_0001.php>

13.　　Johannes Vehlow, *Lehrkurs der wissenschaftlichen Geburts – Astrologie.*1933.

14.　　"Introduction to Astrology" by Al-Qabisi – or Alcabitius – (translated Burnett, Yamamoto and Yamo; Warburg Inst, 2004), mentions the affliction of being in the 'burnt path' in chap III, 150 (p.105).

15.　　Claude Dariot, *A Brief and most easie Introduction to the Astrologicall judgments of the stares.* 1598.

16.　　Agapius (Mahoub) de Menbidj (Trans. Alexandre Vasiliev), "Kitab Al-Unvan Histoire Universelle", *L'antiquité grecque et latine du moyen âge,* 2003, accessed December 2011, < http://remacle.org/bloodwolf/arabe/agapius/histoire.htm#_ftnref16>

17.　　Ibn Ezra (Tr Meira Epstein ed. editor Rob Hand) *The Book of Nativities and Revolutions,* ARHAT, US.

18.   Bernard Goldstein and David Pingree, "Additional Astrological Almanacs from the Cairo Geniza", *Journal of the American Oriental Society*, American Oriental Society, Vol. 103, No. 4 (Oct. - Dec., 1983), pp. 673-690.

19.   Marsilio Ficino, (Tr. Carol V Kaske & John R Clarke), *Three Books on Life*, MRTS, Binghampton, New York, 1989. Book III, Chapter VI, p. 271.

20.   Richard Saunders, *Astrological Judgement and Practice of Physick*. London, 1677, p.63.

21.   Nicholas de Vore, *Encyclopedia of Astrology*. Astrology Center of America: New York, 2005 (reprint of 1947 edition).

22.   Al-Biruni (Tr. R Ramsey Wright), *The Book of Instruction in the Elements of the Art of Astrology*. Luzac: London, 1934, Ch.444.

23.   The Enuma Anu Enlil (In the days of Anu and Enlil) is a series of 68 tablets dealing with Babylonian astrology. It interprets a wide variety of celestial and atmospheric phenomena in terms relevant to the king and state. The tablets themselves were found in the Assyrian king Assurbani-pal's library in the ancient city of Nineveh (modern Tell Kuyunjik, Iraq), and were written in the seventh century BCE. Evidence suggests the collection of omens is much older than the tablets and that the original series probably dates back to the second millennium BCE. The earliest references are found in the incomplete Gu-text, dated between the seventh and fifth centuries BCE.

24.   Francesca Rochberg, *Babylonian Horoscopes*. Philadelphia: American Philosophical society, 1998, pp.46-47.

25.   Rupert Gleadow, *The Origin of the Zodiac*. Jonathan Cape: London, 1968, pp.210-211.

26.   Ed Kahout, "Earth Day, Easter and the Exaltations of the Luminaries", M*undane Astrology*, 2003, accessed January 2012. <edkohout.com/mundane/earthday-02.html>

27.   Chris Brennan, "The Questionable Origins of the Exaltations in Astrology", *The Horoscopic Astrology Blog. 2008*, accessed January 2012. <http://horoscopicastrologyblog.com/2008/11/16/the-questionable-origins-of-the-exaltations-in-astrology/>

28.   Gavin White, "The Exaltation System in Babylonian Astrology", *Skyscript*, 2009, accessed January 2012 <http://www.skyscript.co.uk/exaltations.html>

29.   Ibid.

30.   Joanne Conman, "The Egyptian Origins of Planetary Hypsomata", *Discussions in Egyptology 64*. 2006 -2009, pp. 7-20.

31.   Al-Biruni, (Tr. R Ramsey Wright), *The Book of Instruction in the Elements of the Art of Astrology*. Luzac: London, 1934.

32.   Andrew Bevan, "The Origin of the Planetary Exaltations", Astrologer Andrew J Bevan. 2008, accessed January 2012. ,http://www.astronor.com/exaltations.htm>

33.   Robert Schmidt, "Exaltations", *ACT Astrology*, 2009, accessed January 2012. <http://actastrology.com/viewtopic.php?f=4&t=108&start=10>

34.   Ibid.

35.   Sarah Belle Dougherty, "A Key to Ancient Greece", *World Spiritual Traditions*. Accessed February 2012 <http://www.theosophy-nw.org/theosnw/world/med/me-sbd2.htm>

36.   In line 460 of his *Aratus*.

37.   CE 77, the Roman writer Pliny the Elder, in his book *Natural History*.

38.   Ian Ridpath, "A Brief History of Halley's Comet". Accessed January 2012 <http://www.ianridpath.com/halley/halley1.htm>

39.   Dickson White, Andrew, "New Chapters in the Warfare of Science", *Popular Science Monthly*, October 1885.

40.   Edwin Emerson, *Comet lore, Halley's comet in history and astronomy*. Schilling Press: New York, 1910, accessed January 2012 <http://www.archive.org/stream/cometlorehalleys00emerrich/cometlorehalleys00emerrich_djvu.txt>

41.   Ibid.

42.   Ibid.

43.   Ridpath op. cit.

44.   CE 77, the Roman writer Pliny the Elder, in his book *Natural History*.

45.   Suetonius in his *Life of Caesar*.

46.   Amedee Guillemin (Tr. James Glaishee), *World of Comets*. Sampson Low: London, 1877. Accessed December 2012 <http://www.archive.org/stream/worldofcomets00guiluoft/worldofcomets00guiluoft_djvu.txt>

47.   Charles P Olivier, *Comets*. Bailliere Tindall And Cox:London, 1930. Accessed November 2011 <http://www.archive.org/stream/comets033133mbp/comets033133mbp_djvu.txt>

48.   David N Keightley, "Space Travel in Bronze Age China?", *Skeptical Inquirer*, Volume 3.1, Fall 1978. Accessed January 2012 <http://www.csicop.org/si/show/space_travel_in_bronze_age_china>

49.   Emerson op. cit.

50.   Infoman, "Halley's Comet." Accessed November 2011 <http://infoman16.tripod.com/Articles/halley.htm>

51.   Emerson op. cit.

52.   Christopher Cevasco, "Halley's Comet: Part 2." Accessed November 2011 <http://www.christophermcevasco.com/2011/05/26/halleys-comet-part-ii-1066/>

53.   Jevanji Jamshedji, *Asiatic Papers*. The British India Press: Bombay, 1902. Accessed November 2011 < http://www.archive.org/stream/asiaticpapers035273mbp/asiaticpapers035273mbp_djvu.txt>

54.   Muslim Heritage "Ibn Ridhwan". Accessed November 2011 <http://muslimheritage.com/topics/default.cfm?ArticleID=831>

55.   F R Stephenson, D H Clark and D F Crawford, "The supernova of AD 1006", *Monthly Notices of the Royal Astronomical Society*, Vol. 180, p. 567-584 (1977) Accessed November 2011 <http://adsabs.harvard.edu/full/1977MNRAS.180..567S>

56.   Ovid, *Metamorphoses*. 1. 750 ff: Accessed February 2012 <http://www.perseus.tufts.edu/hopper/text?doc=Perseus%3Atext%3A1999.02.0074%3Abook%3D2>

57.   Plato, *Timaeus*. Eberhard Zanger (Trans.) The Flood from Heaven: Deciphering the Atlantis Legend. William Morrow & Company: 1992.

58.   Ovid op. cit.

59.   Eridanus is the sixth largest constellation and is part of the Heavenly Waters, located between Taurus in the north, Cetus northwest, Fornax and Phoenix southwest, Hydrus to the south and Horologium, Caelum, Lepus and Orion east.

60.   Ovid op. cit.

61.   Apollonius Rhodius (trans. RC Seaton) *Argonautica* 4. 598 ff. Loeb Classical Library: London, 1912.

62.   Aeschylus, *Heliades* (lost play) (Greek tragedy c.5th BCE).

63.   Ovid, "An excerpt from *The Metamorphoses* by Ovid, as translated by A.E. Watts." Accessed February 2012 http://abob.libs.uga.edu/bobk/ovid.html>

64.   Diodorus Siculus, *Library of History* 5. 23. 2 (trans. Oldfather) (Greek historian C1st B.C.) Loeb Classical Library Volumes 303 and 340: London, 1935.

65.   Ovid, *Metamorphoses* 1. 750 ff. Accessed February 2012 <http://www.perseus.tufts.edu/hopper/text?doc=Perseus%3Atext%3A1999.02.0074%3Abook%3D2>

66. Bob Kobres, "Comet Phaethon's Ride". 1993. Accessed February 2012 <http://abob.libs.uga.edu/bobk/phaeth.html>

67. Annals of the Bamboo Book (Ch. 4, part 5) (approx. 1150 BCE). Bob Kobres, "Comet Phaethon's Ride". 1993. Accessed February 2012 <http://abob.libs.uga.edu/bobk/phaeth.html>

68. Aristotle, Meteorology. Accessed February 2012 <http://classics.mit.edu/Aristotle/meteorology.1.i.html>

69. Isaiah 14:12, approx. sixth century BCE.

70. Extract from Eberhard Zanger's translation of Plato's *Timaeus*, from his book *The Flood from Heaven: Deciphering the Atlantis Legend*,William Morrow & Company, 1992

71. Plato (Tr. Thomas Taylor), *The Timaeus*. London, 1793. Accessed November 2011 < http://www.masseiana.org/timaeus.htm>

72. E. Jeffreys, M. Jeffreys and R. Scott. T*he Chronicle of John Malalas*. 1986, Melbourne: Byzantina Australiensia, Australian Assoc. Byzantine Studies 4.

73. Ellen Lloyd, *Voices from Legendary Times*. iUniverse: Lincoln, NE, 2005.

74. John P Pratt, "Astronomical Witnesses of the Great Flood", JohnPratt.com. 2003, accessed February 2012 <http://www.johnpratt.com/items/docs/lds/meridian/2003/deluge.html>

75. Giorgio de Santillana and Hertha von Dechend, *Hamlet's Mill: an Essay on Myth and the Frame of Time*. Godine: Boston: 1977.

76. Manley P Hall, *The Secret Teachings of All Ages*. 1928, accessed February 2012 <http://www.sacred-texts.com/eso/sta/sta12.htm>

77. Lunarium, *Piers Plowman*. Accessed February 2012 <http://www.luminarium.org/medlit/plowman.htm>

78. Penny Drayton, "In Heaven as on Earth", *Royal roads and the Milky Way*. 1995, accessed February 2012 <http://www.indigogroup.co.uk/edge/Royalrds.htm>

79. Ibid.

80. Ibid.

81. Andrei Dorian Gheorghe and Alastair McBeath, "Gheonoaia & Scorpia: More Romanian Dragons", *Cosmo Poetry*. 1998, accessed February 2012 <http://www.cosmopoetry.ro/Romanian%20Astrohumanism%207/Pages/romanian_astrohumanism_VII-4.htm>

82. Genesis 28:12.

83. Lucretius, *De Rerum Natura*, Book 1 Verse 173 (c.95–55 BCE), Routledge: London, 1974.

84.   Robert Chambers, *Chamber's Book of Days*. 1869, accessed February 2012 <http://www.thebookofdays.com/about_bod.htm>

85.   Robert Means Lawrence, *The Magic of the Horse-Shoe*. Houghton, Mifflin and Company: Boston and New York, 1898. Accessed February 2012 <sacred-texts.com/etc/mhs/mhs52.htm>

86.   American Library Institute Papers and Proceedings, Chicago, 1917. Accessed February 2012 <http://www.archive.org/stream/papersandprocee00instgoog/papersandprocee00instgoog_djvu.txt>

87.   *Quran* Sura 10, verse 5.

88.   Daniel Varisco ("Islamic Folk Astronomy." In: Selin, Helaine. (Editor). (2000). *Astronomy Across Cultures.*

89.   Edward C Sachau, *Alberuni's India: an account of the religion, philosophy, and literature*. Trubner: London, 1888, p.277.

90.   George Crabb, *Universal Technological Dictionary*, Baldwin, Cradock & Joy: London, 1851.

91.   Mrs J B Dal, *Indian Palmistry*. Theosophical Publishing Society: Madras, 1895.

92.   Ibid.

93.   Aaron Hill, T*he plain dealer: being select essays on several curious subjects*. London, 1724.

94.   A Table of Palmistry from Saunders",The Astrologer's Magazine and Philosophical Miscellany, Volume 1. London, February 1792.

95.   Executive summary, "An Evaluation of Remote Viewing: Research and Applications", American Institutes for Research, Sept 29 1995.

96.   In a hadith from al-Imam al-Saadiq from *The Islamic Sexual Morality*. Syed Athar Husain and SH Rizvi, *Islamic Marriage A Handbook for Young Muslims*. Mumbai: World Islamic Network, 2001.

97.   University of Glasgow. "Middle English Text on Planting and Grafting in Cambridge, Trinity College, O.5.26", Medical Treatises England: c.1475-1500. http://special.lib.gla.ac.uk/exhibns/month/may2006.html (Accessed 30 November 2011.

98.   Means Lawrence op. cit.

99.   László Sándor Chardonnens *Anglo-Saxon Prognostics, 900-1100*: Study and Texts. Brill: Leiden, Boston, 2007.

100.   John Partridge, *Mikropanastron, or an Astrological Vade Mecum, briefly Teaching the whole Art of Astrology - viz., Questions, Nativities, with all its parts, and the whole Doctrine of Elections never so comprised nor compiled before, &c*. London: William Bromwich, 1679. p.49.

101.   William Eland, *A Tutor to Astrology*. London, 1694.

102.   Henry Coley, *Centiloquium of Hermes Trismegistus in Clavis Astrologiae Elimata* (*Key to the Whole Art of Astrology*). London: 1676.

103.   Bailey op. cit.

104.   John Middleton, *Practical Astrology.* London: 1679, p.97.

105.   Partridge op. cit.

106.   Nicholas Culpeper, *Opus astrologicum*. London: Moone & Steph, 1654.

107.   William Thrasher, *Jubar Astrologicum or a True Astrological Guide*. London:1671.

108.   John Gadbury, *The Doctrine of Nativities & Horary Questions*. Giles Calvert: London, 1658.

109.   de Vore op. cit.

110.   Moxon op. cit.

111.   Vivian Robson, *Electional Astrology*. JP Lippincott: London, 1937.

112.   Simmonite op. cit.

113.   University of Glasgow op. cit.

114.   Means Lawrence op. cit.

115.   Gyer op. cit.

116.   John Fage, *Speculum Aegrotorum*. London, 1606.

117.   Blagrave op. cit.

118.   Nicholas Culpeper, *Opus astrologicum*. London: Moone & Steph, 1654.

119.   Richard Saunders , A*strological Judgement and Practice of Physick*. London, 1671, p.63.

120.   Coley op. cit.

121.   John Gadbury, *Nauticum Astrologicum or The Astrologer's Seaman*. London, 1660.

122.   William Ramesey, *Astrologia Restaurata,* London, 1653.

123.   Ibid.

124.   John Gadbury, *The Doctrine of Nativities & Horary Questions*. Giles Calvert: London, 1658.

125.   WJ Simmonite, *Horary Astrology*. John Story: London, 1896. p.208.

126.   Ramesey op. cit. p.127.

127.   Ibid.

128.   Partridge op. cit.

129.   Paul Christian, *History and Practice of Magic*. Kessinger: 1994. p.582.

130.   Ebenezer Sibly, *A New and Complete Illustration of the Celestial Science of Astrology*. 1795.

131.   Diana Stone, "Questions and Answers", The Fraser Valley Astrological Guild. Accessed January 2012 <http://www.astrologyguild.com/horary1.htm>

132.   Astrology Notes, Via Combusta". *Astrology Notes*: 2006, accessed February 2012 <http://astrologynotes.org/wiki/Via_Combusta>

133.   Lashtal, Home of the Aleister Crowley Society. 1998-2002, accessed December 2011 <www.lashtal.com/nuke/PNphpBB2-printview-t-1205-start-0.phtm

134.   Archie Dunlop, *Elnu*. Accessed December 2011 <http://www.elnu.com/blog/archives/19>

135.   John M Hansen, "Business Astrology 2008-08-12", AFA. Accessed January 2012 <http://www.astrologers.com/news/view-article.php?article_id=10>

136.   Marc Edmund Jones, *Horary Astrology.* Shambala: London, 1975.

137.   Grillot de Givry (Tr. J Courtenay Locke), *Witchcraft, Magic & Alchemy*, Dover Occult: 2009.

138.   Sibly op. cit.

139.   Richard Thomson, *Tales of an Antiquary*. London: Colburn & R. Bentley: London, 1828, p.146.

Sources

Introduction

RG Aitken , "The Zodiacal Constellation Scorpio", *Publications of the Astronomical Society of the Pacific*, Vol. 36, No. 211, p. 124.

Al Biruni, R. Ramsay Wright (Trans.) *The Book of Instruction in the Elements of the Art of Astrology.* Kessinger: USA, 2010.

U Dallolmo, "Latin Terminology Relating to Aurorae, Comets, Meteors and Novae", *Journal for the History of Astronomy*, V1.1 p.10 1980.

1- Location, location, location

Al Biruni, R. Ramsay Wright (Trans.) T*he Book of Instruction in the Elements of the Art of Astrology.* Kessinger: USA, 2010.

Abu Ma'shar (tr. Charles Burnett) *Abreviation of the Introduction to Astrology,* ARHAT, US .

Alcabitius *Introduction to Astrology* by Al-Qabisi or Alcabitius, (translated Burnett, Yamamoto and Yamo) Warburg Institute: London, 2004.

Robert Ambelain, *Traité d'Astrologie Esoterique*, Éditions Adyar, Paris, 1937. *Astrologischer Auskunftsbogen,* July 1962.

Nathan Bailey, *An Universal Etymological English Dictionary. London*, 1737.

Francis Barrett, *The Magus.* London, 1801.

Joseph Blagrave, *Astrological Practice of Physick*, London, 1671.

Frederico Capone, "La Via Combusta", FISA, accessed 1 January 2012. <http://fisa.altervista.org/via_combusta.html >.

Centiloquium of Hermes Trismegistus, accessed January 2012 <http://www.classicalastrologer.com/centiloquium_of_hermes_trismegis.htm>

Elisha Coles, *An English Dictionary Explaining the Difficult Terms that are Used*, London, 1677.

Fabrizio Corrias, *DIGNITÀ E DEBILITÀ PLANETARIE ESSENZIALI*, Almugea, Scuola di Astrologia. Undated.

Nicholas Culpeper, *Opus astrologicum*. London, 1654.

Claude Dariot, *A Brief and most easie Introduction to the Astrologicall judgments of the stares.* 1598.

Dorotheus of Sidon, *Carmen Astrologicum.* Astrology Classics: New York, 2005 (reprint of 1976 edition), p.265.

Ben Dykes, *Bonnatti's Book of Astronomy* (Trans.). Cazimi Press: 2010.

esotericism.ro, *Astrological Glossary*, accessed January 2012, <http://www.

esoterism.ro/english/astrological-glossary.php>

Ibn Ezra (Tr Meira Epstein ed. editor Rob Hand) *The Book of Nativities and Revolutions*, ARHAT, US.

John Fage, *Speculum Aegrotorum*. London, 1606 .

Auger Ferrier, *Des jugemens astronomiques sur les nativitez*. [Translated from the Latin.] Lyon, 1550.

Marsilio Ficino, (Tr. Carol V Kaske & John R Clarke), *Three Books on Life*, MRTS, Binghampton, New York, 1989.

Juan De Figueroa, *Opúsculo de Astrología*. Lima, 1660.

Ian Freer,"The Picatrix: Lunar Mansions in Western Astrology". Astrological Association, accessed 4 September 2011, <http://www.astrologer.com/aanet/pub/journal/picatrix.html>

John Gadbury, *Genethlialogia*. London, 1658.

James Holden, *A History of Horoscopic Astrology*. American Federation of Astrologers: USA, 1996.

John Gadbury, *The Doctrine of Nativities & Horary Questions*. Giles Calvert: London, 1658.

Luca Gaurico e l'astrologia a Mantova nella prima metà del cinquecento. (Estratto da L'Archiginnasio.) <http://www.treccani.it/enciclopedia/luca-gaurico_%28Dizionario-Biografico%29/> accessed November 2011.

Bernard Goldstein and David Pingree, "Additional Astrological Almanacs from the Cairo Geniza", *Journal of the American Oriental Society, American Oriental Society*, Vol. 103, No. 4 (Oct. - Dec., 1983), pp. 673-690.

John Mason Good, Olinthus Gregory and Newton Bosworth, *Pantologia*, London, 1813.

Henri Gouchon, *Dictionnaire d'Astrologie*. Dervy, Paris, 1937.

Nicholas Gyer, *The English Phlebotomy*. London, 1592.

James Holden, *History of Horoscopic Astrology*. American Federation of Astrologers: US, 2006.

Randle Holme, *The Academy of Armory*. London, 1688.

Erwin Huizenga, "Die 100 capittelen van astronomijen. Tekst en traditie van een Middelnederlands astrologisch traktaat". *Scientiarum historia 16* (1990), no. 1-2, pp. 29-55.

Marc Edmund Jones, *Problem Solving by Horary Astrology*. Aurora press: US, 1993.

John Kersey, *A New World of Words*. London, 1706.

Lee Lehman, John Partridge, *Mikropanastron, or an Astrological Vade Mecum*, accessed December 2011, <www.leelehman.com/pages/images/Partridge.doc>

William Lilly, *Christian Astrology*. London, 1647.

Linguaggio Astrale dal 1970. Trimestrale del Centro Italiano di Discipline Astrologiche: Primavera 2006.

Anthony Louis, *Horary Astrology Plain and Simple*, Llewellyn: US, 1998.

Jean Jacques Manget, *Bibliotheca pharmaceutico-medica, seu rerum ad pharmaciam galenico-chymicam*. Geneva, 1704.

Henrike Mayer, "Via Combusta", *The Astrological Journal*. Astrological Association: UK, May/Jun 2007.

Maurice McCann, "Via Combusta in Astrology" The Astrologers" *Quarterly Vol. 61* no 2. Astrological Lodge of London: London, 1987.

Agapius (Mahoub) de Menbidj (Trans. Alexandre Vasiliev), "Kitab Al-Unvan Histoire Universelle", L'antiquité grecque et latine du moyen âge, 2003, accessed December 2011 < http://remacle.org/bloodwolf/arabe/agapius/histoire.htm#_ftnref16>

John Middleton, *Practical Astrology.* London, 1678, p.97.

Joseph Moxon, *Mathematicks Made Easy.* London 1679.

John Partridge, *Mikropanastron: or an Astrological Vade Mecum*, London, 1679.

Edward Phillips, *The New World of English Words.* London, 1658.

Giovanni Battista Carello Piacentino, *Le Efemeridi per anni 17 al meridiano della inclita Citta' di Vinegia diligentissimamente calcolate, nella prima parte delle quali si discorrono minutamente molte cose di astrologia,* Vinegia, 1555.

William Ramesey, *Astrologia Restaurata,* London, 1653, p.127.

Vivian Robson, *Electional Astrology.* JP Lippincott: Philadelphia, 1937.

Jorg Sabellicus, *Heptameron di Pietro D'Abano.* Hermes: Italy, 1984.

Richard Saunders, *Astrological Judgement and Practice of Physick.* London, 1671.

WJ Simmonite, *The Complete Arcana of Astral Philosophy.* London, 1890, p28.

Johannes Vehlow *Lehrkurs der wissenschaftlichen Geburts - Astrologie.* 1933.

Antoine de Villion, *L'usage des Éphémérides, avec la méthode de dresser et corriger toute sorte de figures cœlestes, etc.* Paris, 1624.

Nicholas de Vore, *Encyclopedia of Astrology.* Astrology Center of America: New York, 2005 (reprint of 1947 edition).

George Wharton, *The works of that late most excellent philosopher and astronomer, Sir George Wharton, bar. collected into one volume by John Gadbury.* London, 1683.

2 - AVERAGES

William Frederic Badae, *The Old Testament in the Light of To-Day: A Study in Moral Development.* Houghton Mifflin Company: Boston, 1915.

Hermann Hunger & David Pingree, *Astral Sciences in Mesopotamia.* BRILL: 1999.

Morris Jastrow Jr, "Hebrew and Babylonian Traditions" *The Haskell Lectures, Delivered at Oberlin College in 1913.* Charles Scribner's Sons: New York, 1914.

John D Keyser, "From Sabbath to Saturday: The Story of the Jewish Rest Day", Hope of Israel Ministries. Accessed February 2012 < http://hope-of-israel.org/sabtosat.htm>

Samuel Macauley Jackson (Ed.), *The New Schaff-Herzog Encyclopedia of Religious Knowledge Volume 10.* Funk and Wagnalls: New York, 1911.

E G Richards, *Mapping Time: The Calendar and Its History.* Oxford University Press: Oxford, 1999.

John Edwin Sandys, *Companion to Latin Studies*. Cambridge University Press: Cambridge, 1913.

William Smith & Charles Anthon, A *School Dictionary of Greek and Roman Antiquities*. Harper and Brothers: New York, 1857.

Sacha Stern, Calendar and Community: A *History of the Jewish Calendar, Second Century BCE-Tenth Century CE*. Oxford University Press: Oxford, 2001.

Roland de Vaux (author) & John McHugh (Trans.) A*ncient Israel: Its Life and Institutions*. McGraw-Hill: New York, 1961.

3 - BEING DIGNIFIED

"The origin of Exaltations and Rulerships", Skyscript. 2009, Accessed February 2012 <http://skyscript.co.uk/forums/viewtopic.php?t=4554>

"Specific and Malefic Degrees" Mithras Astrology. 2002, accessed February 2012 <http://mithras93.tripod.com/lessons/lesson5/index.html>

"Vedic Astrology Lessons", astrojyoti.com. Accessed January 2012 <http://www.astrojyoti.com/lesson6.htm>

Abû Ma'sar, (Italian trans. Giuseppe Bezza, English trans. Daria Dudziak) *Libri mysteriorum. Cielo e Terra*. Accessed February 2012 < http://www.cieloeterra.it/eng/eng.testi.metafore/eng.metafore.html>

ACT Astrology. 2009, accessed February 2012 <http://actastrology.com/viewtopic.php?f=4&t=108>

Astrogeographia, 2007, accessed December 2011 <http://www.astrogeographia.org/about_us/>

Heinrich Cornelius Agrippa, *Of Occult Philosophy, Book II*. (Part 3), accessed February 2012 <http://www.esotericarchives.com/agrippa/agripp2c.htm>

Antiquuus Astrology 2007 accessed 12 January 2012 <http://www.antiquus-astrology.com/Chap2-14.html>

Astrojyoti "Brihat Parashara Hora Sashtra by Rishi Parashara",accessed 12 January 2012 <http://www.astrojyoti.com/bphspage1.htm>

Tamsyn Barton, *Ancient Astrology*. Routledge: New York, 1994.

Roger Beck, *A Brief History of Ancient Astrology*. Blackwell Publishing: Oxford, 2007

Andrew Bevan, "The Origin of the Planetary Exaltations", Astrologer Andrew J Bevan. 2008, accessed January 2012 <http://www.astronor.com/exaltations.htm>

Al-Biruni, (Tr. R Ramsey Wright), The Book of Instruction in the Elements of the Art of Astrology. Luzac: London, 1934.

Chris Brennan, "The Questionable Origins of the Exaltations in Astrology", *The Horoscopic Astrology Blog*. 2008, accessed January 2012 <http://horoscopicastrologyblog.com/2008/11/16/the-questionable-origins-of-the-exaltations-in-astrology/>

Chris Brennan, "The Thema Mundi", *The Horoscopic Astrology Blog*. 2007, accessed January 2012 <http://horoscopicastrologyblog.com/2007/06/11/the-thema-mundi/>

Andrew Carter, "A Closer Look at Exaltation (4)", *Altair Astrology*, 3

November 2006, accessed January 2012 <http://altairastrology.wordpress.com/2006/11/03/a-closer-look-at-exaltation-4/>

Joanne Conman, "The Egyptian Origins of Planetary Hypsomata", *Discussions in Egyptology 64*. 2006 -2009, pp. 7-20.

Joanne Conman, "Origins of Astrology", 2010 accessed January 2012 <http://www.kepler.edu/home/index.php?option=com_content&view=article&id=324:origins-of-astrology&catid=60:newsletter-articles&Itemid=157>

Cyril Fagan, *Zodiacs, Old and New*. Anscombe: 1951.

Frederick Leigh Gardner, *Bibliotheca Astrologica*. London, 1903.

Garg, Dr. Arjun Kumar, "Rahu-Ketu", *Future Point Astro Solutions*, accessed 12 January 2012 <http://www.futurepointindia.com/articles/research-articles/rahu-ketu.aspx>

Thomas Gerard, "More on the Terms or Bounds" *Altair Astrology*. 2009, accessed February 2012 <http://altairastrology.wordpress.com/2009/02/24/termsbounds-and-appearance/>

Rupert Gleadow, *The Origin of the Zodiac*. Jonathan Cape: London, 1968.

Robert Hand, "Dignities and Debilities as Collected from a Variety of Sources", ARHAT Publications: 1998-2010, accessed February 2012 <http://www.arhatmedia.com/alldign.htm>

John Major Jenkins, "The Solstice Gateways and the Polar-to-Solar Shift", Alignment2012.com. 2002, accessed January 2012 <http://www.alignment2012.com/polar-to-solar.html>

Alexander Jones and John M Steel, "A New Discovery of a Component of Greek Astrology in Babylonian Tablets: the 'Terms'", *ISAW Papers 1 (2011)*. 2011, accessed January 2012 <http://dlib.nyu.edu/awdl/isaw/isaw-papers/1/>

Marc Edmund Jones, *Horary Astrology*. Shambala: London, 1975.

Ed Kahout, "Earth Day, Easter and the Exaltations of the Luminaries", *Mundane Astrology*, 2003, accessed January 2012 <edkohout.com/mundane/earthday-02.html>

Curtis Manwaring, "Hellenistic case for Evolutionary Astrology", *The Lost Horoscope X Files*. 2010, Accessed January 2012 <http://www.astrology-x-files.com/x-files/evolutionary-astro.html>

Maurice McCann, "Considerations before Judgement", Astrology - The Astrologers' Quarterly, Vol. 61 no 2. Astrological Lodge of London: London, Summer 1987.

Julius Firmicus Maternus (Jean Rhys Bram) A*ncient Astrology Theory and Practice*, Astrology Center of America: New York, 2005.

Lester Ness, Astrology and Judaism in Late Antiquity. 1993, accessed January 2012 <http://www.smoe.org/arcana/diss2.html>

Otto Neugebauer and Richard A. Parker, *Egyptian Astronomical Texts Volume III*. Brown University Press: Providence, RI, 1969.

Robert Powell, *History of the Zodiac*. Sophia Academic Press: 2006.

Robert Powell, "The Significance of Mega Stars", *Christian Star Calendar. 2008*, accessed January 2012 <http://www.astrogeographia.org/significance_of_mega_stars>

Francesca Rochberg, *Babylonian Horoscopes*. Philadelphia: American Philosophical society, 1998.

Robert Schmidt, "Exaltations", ACT Astrology, 2009, accessed January 2012 <http://actastrology.com/viewtopic.php?f=4&t=108&start=10>

Shlomo Sela, *Abraham Ibn Ezra and the Rise of Medieval Hebrew Science*. Brill: Boston, 2003.

Jim Tester, A History of Western Astrology. Boydell & Brewer: London, 1987.

Prashant Trivedi, *The Key of Life: Astrology of the Lunar Nodes*. Lotus Brands: Twin Lakes, WI, 2002.

Vedic Astrology Net "Brihat Parashara Hora Shastra", accessed 12 January 2012, <http://vedic-astrology.net/Articles/Brihat-Parashara-Hora-Shastra.asp>

Nicholas de Vore, *Encyclopedia of Astrology*. Astrology Center of America: New York, 2005 (reprint of 1947 edition).

Gavin White, "The Exaltation System in Babylonian Astrology", Skyscript, 2009, accessed January 2012 <http://www.skyscript.co.uk/exaltations.html>

4 - Give me a sign

"Antares in Scorpio", SouledOut.Org, accessed February 2012 <http://souledout.org/cosmology/highlights/antares/antares.html>

"Scorpion", Khandro net.Accessed February 2012 <http://www.khandro.net/animal_scorpion.htm>

Heinrich Cornelius Agrippa, *Of Occult Philosophy, Book II*. (part 3). Accessed February 2012 <http://www.esotericarchives.com/agrippa/agripp2c.htm>

Richard Hinchley Allen, *Star Names: Their Lore and Meaning*. Dover Publications: London, 1889/1963.

S H Dewdney, "The Zodiac and Early Astronomy", *Journal of the Royal Astronomical Society of Canada*, Vol. 25. 1931.

Sarah Belle Dougherty, "A Key to Ancient Greece", *World Spiritual Traditions*. Accessed February 2012 < http://www.theosophy-nw.org/theosnw/world/med/me-sbd2.htm>

Kathleen Freeman, A*ncilla to the Pre-Socratic Philosophers*. 1948, accessed February 2012 < http://www.sacred-texts.com/cla/app/>

Mary Grant (trans.), *The Myths of Hyginus*. University of Kansas Publications in Humanistic Studies, no. 34. University of Kansas Press: Lawrence, 1960.

Thomas Little Heath, *A History of Greek Mathematics: From Thales to Euclid*, Volume 1. Dover: US, 1981.

Anthony Hope, "Primary Sources", *A Guide to Ancient Near Eastern Astronomy*. Accessed February 2012 <http://www.astronomy.pomona.edu/archeo/outside/primary.html>

Deborah Houlding, "Heavenly Imprints. 1997", accessed February 2012 <http://www.skyscript.co.uk/zodiachistory_print.html>

Deborah Houlding, "Scorpio the Scorpion", Skyscript. Accessed February 2012 <http://www.skyscript.co.uk/scorpio_myth.html>

Jean-Charles Houzeau and Albert Benoît Marie Lancaster, *Bibliographie générale de l'astronomie*. L'Academie Royale de Belgique: Brussells, 1887.

Alexander del Mar, *Worship of Augustus Caesar*. Cambridge Encyclopedia Company: New York, 1900.

Lester Ness, *Astrology and Judaism in Late Antiquity*. 1993, accessed January 2012 <http://www.smoe.org/arcana/diss2.html>

Robert Powell, History of the Zodiac. Sophia Academic Press: 2006.

William Ramsay, "Astronomia", A *Dictionary of Greek and Roman Antiquities*. John Murray: London, 1875, accessed February 2012 <http://penelope.uchicago.edu/Thayer/E/Roman/Texts/secondary/SMIGRA*/Astronomia.html>

Gary D Thompson, "Essays Relating To The History Of Occidental Constellations and Star Names to the Classical Period", *The Origin of the Zodiac. 2001-2011*, accessed February 2012 <http://members.westnet.com.au/gary-david-thompson/page9a.html>

Anne Wright, "Scorpius", Constellations of Words. Accessed February 2012 <http://www.constellationsofwords.com/Constellations/Scorpio.html>

WilliamThrasher, *Jubar Astrologicum or a True Astrological Guide*. London:1671.

University of Glasgow. "Middle English Text on Planting and Grafting in Cambridge, Trinity College, O.5.26", Medical Treatises England: c.1475-1500. Accessed 30 November 2011 <http://special.lib.gla.ac.uk/exhibns/month/may2006.html>

Nicholas de Vore, *Encyclopedia of Astrology*. Astrology Classics Publishing: New York, 2005 (1947 facsimile).

5 - SHOOTING STARS

2008 Pecos Conference Research Articles, accessed January 2012 <http://www.swanet.org/2008_pecos_conference/related.html>

Astronomy 2011 Singapore, "The Far Side of Astronomy: Culture", accessed January 2012 <ttp://earthstar.htmlplanet.com/farside_culture.htm>

Marguerite Boardman, "The Constellation Scorpio, also Planet Notes for July, August and September" *Publication of the Pomona College Astronomical Society, vol. 4*, 1915, pp.157-161. Accessed January 2012 <1915PPCAS...4..157B>

William Patrick Bourne, "The Chinese "Guest Star" of 1054 AD and Earth Catastrophism", 2002, Accessed January 2012 <http://www.darkstar1.co.uk/williambourne.html>

John C Brandt, Robert DeWitt Chapman, *Introduction to Comets*. Cambridge University Press: Cambridge, 2004.

Robert Burnham, *Great Comets*. Cambridge University Press: Cambridge, 2000.

J R Collins, "New Stars", *Journal of the Royal Astronomical Society of Canada Vol.15*, No.3,, 1921, accessed January 2012 <http://adsabs.harvard.edu/full/1921JRASC..15...89C>

D Cook, "A Survey of Muslim Material on Comets and Meteors", *Journal for the History of Astronomy*, p.131. 1999.

U Dallolmo, "Latin Terminology Relating to Aurorae, Comets, Meteors and Novae", *Journal for the History of Astronomy*, V1.1 p.10 1980, accessed January 2012 <http://articles.adsabs.harvard.edu/full/1980JHA....11...10D>

Philip M Dauber and Richard A. Muller, *The Three Big Bangs: Comet Crashes, Exploding Stars, and the Creation of the Universe*. Perseus Books: Cambridge, MA, 1996.

Ignatius Donnelly, *Ancient World Wide Legends of the Comet*. Kessinger: 2005.

Henry W Elson. *Comets, Their Origin, Nature and History*. Sturgis and Walton:1910. Accessed 11 January 2012 <http://www.archive.org/stream/cometstheirorigi00elsorich/cometstheirorigi00elsorich_djvu.txt>

Edwin Emerson, *Comet Lore, Halley's comet in history and astronomy*. Schilling Press: New York, 1910, accessed January 2012 <http://www.archive.org/stream/cometlorehalleys00emerrich/cometlorehalleys00emerrich_djvu.txt>

Jonathan Flannery, "Unexpected Visitors: The Theory of the Influence of Comets, accessed January 2012 < http://www.skyscript.co.uk/comet.html>

Dr J K Fotheringham, "The new star of Hipparchus, and the dates of the birth and accession of Mithridates", accessed January 2012 <http://adsabs.harvard.edu/full/1919MNRAS..79..162F>

Ann Geneva, *Astrology and the Seventeenth Century Mind*. Manchester University Press: Manchester, 1995.

Bernard R Goldstein, "Evidence for a Supernova of A. D. 1006", *Astronomical Journal*, Vol. 70, p.139, accessed January 2012 <http://articles.adsabs.harvard.edu/full/1965AJ.....70..139G>

Daniel W Graham and Eric Hintz "An Ancient Greek Sighting of Halley's Comet?" *Journal of Cosmology* Vol. 9 July 2010, accessed January 2012 <http://journalofcosmology.com/AncientAstronomy106.html>

David Green and F Richard Stephenson, "The Historical Supernovae", Supernovae and Gamma Ray Busters, 2003, accessed January 2012 <http://arxiv.org/PS_cache/astro-ph/pdf/0301/0301603v1.pdf>

H S Green, Raphael and Charles E O Carter, *Mundane Astrology*. Astrology Classics: New York, 2004.

Kim Harper, *A Students Guide to Earth Science V1*. Greenwood Press: London, 2004.

Gerald S Hawkins, *Mindsteps to the Cosmos*. Harper & Row: New York, 1983.

Heaven astroloabe, "Johannes Lydus on comets", accessed January 2012 <http://heavenastrolabe.net/johannes-lydus-on-comets/>

Craig Hipkins, "Fireballs: A History of Meteors and other Astronomic Phenomena" Accessed January 2012 <http://www.fireballhistory.com/Ancient-Fireball-Sightings.html>

Karel Van Der Hucht, *Highlights of Astronomy Volume 14*. Cambridge University Press: Cambridge, 2007.

Colin Humphreys, "The Star of Bethlehem", *Science and Christian Belief*, Vol 5, October 1995, accessed January 2012 <http://www.asa3.org/ASA/

topics/Astronomy-Cosmology/S&CB%2010-93Humphreys.html>

Victoria Jaggard, "Ancient Greeks Made First Halley's Comet Sighting?" *National Geographic News*, September 13, 2010, accessed January 2012 < http://newswatch.nationalgeographic.com/2010/09/13/comet_halley_first_sighting_greeks/>

S J Johnson, "Correspondence - Remarks on Comets", *Astronomical Register*, Vol. 18. pp.316-317. Accessed January 2012 <http://articles.adsabs.harvard.edu/full/1880AReg...18..316J>

Keele Astrophysics Group, "Everything you need to know about COMETS" accessed January 2012 <http://www.astro.keele.ac.uk/workx/comets/index2.html>

David N Keightley, "Space Travel in Bronze Age China?", Skeptical Inquirer, Volume 3.1, Fall 1978. Accessed January 2012 <http://www.csicop.org/si/show/space_travel_in_bronze_age_china>

David H Kelley and E F Milone, *Exploring Ancient Skies*. Springer: New York, 2005.

Charles A Kofoid and Prudence W Kofoid, *Pliny's Natural History in Thirty-Seven Books*. Wernerian Club: 1847. Accessed January 2012 <http://archive.org/stream/plinysnaturalhis00plinrich/plinysnaturalhis00plinrich_djvu.txt>

Gary W Kronk, *Cometeography Volume 1: Ancient-1799*. Cambridge University Press: Cambridge, 1999.

Werner Landgraf, *On the Motion of Comet Halley*. Max Planck-Instituit fur Aeronomie: Lindaue, 1984.

James Legge, *The Shû King, Shih King and Hsiâo King: Sacred Books of the East*, Vol. 3, 1879, accessed January 2012 <http://www.sacred-texts.com/cfu/sbe03/sbe03006.htm>

Paul Murdin and Lesley Murdin, *Supernovae*. Cambridge University Press: Cambridge, 1985.

David H Levy, *The Quest for Comets: An Explosive Trail of Beauty and Danger*. Plenum Press: New York, 1994.

Michael Loewe, *Divination, Mythology and Monarchy in Han China*. Cambridge University Press: Cambridge, 1994.

Laurence A Marschall, *The Supernova Story*. Princeton University Press: Chichester, 1988.

C S Mundt, "Notable Astronomers of Past Ages. I-Hipparchus", *Publications of the Astronomical Society of the Pacific*, Vol. 39, No. 227, p.41. (PASP Homepage) 02/1927

NASA, "A Brief History of High-Energy Astronomy", accessed January 2012, <http://heasarc.nasa.gov/docs/heasarc/headates/0.html>

NASA Deep Impact, "Comets in Ancient Cultures", accessed Decenber 2012 <http://www.nasa.gov/mission_pages/deepimpact/media/f_ancient.html>

RL Newburn (Ed.), M. Neugebauer (Ed.) and Jürgen H. Rahe (Ed.) *Comets in the Post Halley Era*: Astrophysics and Space Science Library. Kluwer Academic: Dordrecht, NL, 1991.

Graham Phillips, *Brush with Oblivion*. Accessed January 2012 <http://www.grahamphillips.net/eden/eden_5.htm>

Deborah Lynne Porter, *Deluge to Discourse: Myth, History, and the Generation of Chinese Fiction.* State University of New York Press: New York, 1996.

Ian Ridpath, "A Brief History of Halley's Comet". Accessed January 2012 <http://www.ianridpath.com/halley/halley1.htm>

Ian Ridpath, "Star Tales: Scorpius, the Scorpion, accessed January 2012 <http://www.ianridpath.com/startales/scorpius.htm>

Paul Rincon, "Halley's comet 'was spotted by the ancient Greeks'" 20 September 2012, accessed January 2012, <"http://www.bbc.co.uk/news/science-environment-11255168>

A H Sayce, *Records of the Past,* 2nd series, Vol. I, accessed January 2012, < http://www.sacred-texts.com/ane/rp/rp201/>

S J Schechner, *Comets, Popular Culture, and the Birth of Modern Cosmology.* Princeton University Press: New York, 1997.

Joseph Sherman, *Asteroids, Meteors, and Comets.* Marshall Cavendish: New York, 2010.

Edward Singleton Holden, "Ancient Comets", *Publications of the Astronomical Society of the Pacific,* 4 (1892), 266, accessed January 2012, < http://adsbit.harvard.edu/full/seri/PASP./0004/0000266.000.html>

Skyscript Astrology Forum, "Star of Bethlehem" accessed January 2012 http://skyscript.co.uk/forums/viewtopic.php?t=4992&postdays=0&postorder=asc&highlight=comet&start=15

Space Daily, "Scientists Say Comet Smashed Into Southern Germany In 200 BC" 15 October 2004, Paris, accessed January 2012 <http://www.spacedaily.com/news/comet-04l.html>

F Richard Stephenson and David A Green, "A reappraisal of some proposed historical supernovae", *Journal for the History of Astronomy,* Vol. 36, Part 2, No. 123, p. 217 - 229 (2005), accessed January 2012 <http://articles.adsabs.harvard.edu/full/2005JHA....36..217S>

F R Stephenson and K K C Yau, "Astronomical Records in the Chun-Chiu Chronicle", *Journal for the History of Astronomy,* Vol.23, NO. 1/FEB, P. 31, 1992, accessed January 2012 <http://adsabs.harvard.edu/full/1992JHA....23...31S>

F R Stephenson and D A Green, "A reappraisal of some proposed historical supernovae", *Journal for the History of Astronomy.* Vol. 36, Part 2, No. 123, p. 217 - 229 (2005), accessed January 2012 <http://articles.adsabs.harvard.edu/full/2005JHA....36..217S/0000229.000.html>

Suburban Emergency Management project, "Stones Falling from the Sky, Part I: 1,400 B.C.-1860 A.D.", 2007, accessed December 2012 <"http://www.semp.us/publications/biot_reader.php?BiotID=452>

Wen Shion Tsu , "The observations of Halley's comet in Chinese history", *Popular Astronomy,* Vol. 42, p.191 00/1934.

UCLA Division of Astronomy and Astrophysics, "Comet Misconceptions", accessed January 2012 <http://www.astro.ucla.edu/~kaisler/articles/event_horizon/cometmisc.html>

Mike Wall, "Halley's Comet was Spotted by Ancient Greeks",14 September 2012, accessed January 2012 <http://www.space.com/9116-halley-comet-spotted-ancient-greeks.html>

Michael Windelspecht, *Groundbreaking Scientific Experiments, Inventions and Discoveries of the 17th Century.* Greenwood Press: Westport, CT, 2002.

Anne Wright, "Scorpio", Constellations of Words. Accessed January 2012 <http://www.constellationsofwords.com/Constellations/Scorpio.html>

Zhenoao Xu, W. Pankenier and Yaotiao Jiang, East-Asian Archaeoastronomy: Historical Records of Astronomical Observations of China, Japan and Korea. CRC Press: New York, 2000.

Z Xu, D W Pankenier and Y Jiang, "East Asian Archaeoastronomy", From the collection of Garrett P. Serviss: 2000.

Ho Peng-Yoke, "Ancient and Mediaeval Observations of Comets and Novae in Chinese Sources", *Vistas in Astronomy*, 5 (1962).

Ho Peng Yoke, An Introduction to Science and Civilization in China. Hong Kong University Press: Hong Kong, 1985.

Xi Zezong, "A New Catalog of Novae Recorded in the Chinese and Japanese Chronicles", *Soviet Astronomy, 1* (1957), accessed January 2012 <http://articles.adsabs.harvard.edu/full/seri/SvA../0001/0000161.000.html>

H Zhongwei, R Jinyi, J Guo, H Xianliang and X Dengli, "A Chinese Observing Site from Remote Antiquity", Journal for the History of Astronomy, p.231, accessed January 2012 <1999JHA....30..231Z>

6 - GIVE IT TO THE GREEKS

"Curriculum Materials: World Mythology", *World Mythology in Art.* Accessed February 2012 <http://scholar.cc.emory.edu:80/scripts/APA/abstracts/zissos.html>

"Phaethon's Bolide", *Frontiers of Anthropology.* 2011, accessed February 2012 <http://frontiers-of-anthropology.blogspot.com/2011_07_01_archive.html>

John Ackerman, "Mythology- Greek", *Firmanent and Chaos.* Accessed February 2012 <http://www.firmament-chaos.com/mythology_greek.html>

Aristotle, *Meteorology.* Accessed February 2012 <http://classics.mit.edu/Aristotle/meteorology.1.i.html>

Aaron J. Atsma, "Phaethon", Theoi Project. Accessed February 2012 <http://www.theoi.com/Titan/Phaethon.html>

Sally Corbett and James Parks, "Phaethon and the Chariot of the Sun", *Introduction to Ancient Greece.* 1997, accessed February 2012 <http://www.hipark.austin.isd.tenet.edu/mythology/Phaethon.html>

Department of Classics, Tufts University, Perseus Digital Library. <http://www.perseus.tufts.edu/cgi-bin/text?lookup=encyclopedia+Phaethon>

Bob Kobres, "Oops." Accessed February 2012 < http://abob.libs.uga.edu/bobk/>

Bob Kobres, "Comet Phaethon's Ride". 1993. Accessed February 2012 <http://abob.libs.uga.edu/bobk/phaeth.html>

James Innell Packer and Sven Soderlund,The Way of Wisdom: Essays in Honor of Bruce K. Waltke. Zondervan: Michigan, US, 2000.

Plato *Timaeus*. Eberhard Zanger (Trans.) The Flood from Heaven: Deciphering the Atlantis Legend. William Morrow & Company: US, 1992.

John Lash, "Myths in Metahistory, Metahistory.org. "2002, revised 2009, accessed February 2012 <http://www.metahistory.org/guidelines/MythMetahistory.php>

Timo Niroma, "The Myth of Phaethon", T*he Myth History of the Catastrophe Events and Their Cultural Effects*. Accessed February 2012 <http://personal.eunet.fi/pp/tilmari/tilmari4.htm#phaethon>

Ovid, "An excerpt from The Metamorphoses by Ovid, as translated by A.E. Watts." Accessed February 2012 <http://abob.libs.uga.edu/bobk/ovid.html>

Ovid, *Metamorphoses*. Accessed February 2012 http://www.perseus.tufts.edu/hopper/text?doc=Perseus%3Atext%3A1999.02.0074%3Abook%3D2

Diodorus Siculus, *Library of History* 5. 23. 2 (trans. Oldfather) (Greek historian C1st B.C.) Loeb Classical Library Volumes 303 and 340: London, 1935.

7 - A Long Time Ago

Alan A Alford, "Atlantis, accessed January 2012 <http://www.eridu.co.uk/Author/atlantis/greek.html>

Nigel Blair, "The Search for Atlantis. Access January 2012 <http://www.bibliotecapleyades.net/atlantida_mu/esp_atlantida_6.htm>

Robert Roy Britt, "Comets, Meteors & Myth: New Evidence for Toppled Civilizations and Biblical Tales", Rense.com. Accessed January 2012 < http://www.rense.com/general16/cometsmeteorsandmyth.htm>

Greg Bryant, "The Dark Ages: Were They Darker Than We Imagined?" Accessed January 2012 <http://gchbryant.tripod.com/Articles/darkages0999.htm>

Scott Carney, "Did a Comet Cause the Great Flood?" Discover Magazine. Accessed January 2012. From the November 2007 issue; published online November 15, 2007 <http://discovermagazine.com/2007/nov/did-a-comet-cause-the-great-flood>

S V M Clube, "The Fundamental Role of Giant Comets in Earth History", accessed January 2012 < http://tinyurl.com/c443smd >

Christopher Cullen, Astronomy and mathematics in ancient China: the Zhou bi suan jing. Cambridge University Press: Cambridge, 1996.

Leroy Ellenberger, "An Antidote to Velikovskian Delusions", accessed January 2012 <http://abob.libs.uga.edu/bobk/velidelu.html>

Faithfreedom.org "Apocalypse Forever: The Root of Islam Was a Very Dark Year"accessed January 2012 <http://www.faithfreedom.org/Articles/MarkTwain40627.htm>

Ravindra Godbole, "A Review of Research on Taurids and Meteoric Showers" *The Meaning of Vedas*. Accessed January 2012, <http://www.themeaningofvedas.com/CHAPTER%202.htm>

Bernard R Goldstein, "Evidence for a Supernova of A. D. 1006", *Astronomical Journal*, Vol. 70, p.139, accessed January 2012 <http://articles.adsabs.harvard.edu/full/1965AJ.....70..139G>

Craig Hipkins, "Fireballs: A History of Meteors and other Astronomic Phenomena" Accessed January 2012 <http://www.fireballhistory.com/Ancient-Fireball-Sightings.html>

Harold Jacoby, *Practical Talks by an Astronomer.* Charles Scribner's Sons: New York, 1902. Accessed January 2012 <http://www.archive.org/stream/practicaltalksby00jacouoft/practicaltalksby00jacouoft_djvu.txt>

Jaws of Death, 2000 accessed January 2012 <http://petragrail.tripod.com/jaws.html>

David H Kelley and E F Milone, *Exploring Ancient Skies: An Encyclopedic Survey of Archaeoastronomy.* Springer: New York, 2005.

Thomas F King, "Recent Cosmic Impacts on Earth", Accessed January 2012 <http://archaeology.about.com/od/climatechange/a/masse_king_4.htm>

Bob Kobres, "Comets and the Bronze Age Collapse", accessed January 2012 <http://abob.libs.uga.edu/bobk/bronze.html>

Bob Kobres, "Comet Phaethon's Ride" 1993, accessed January 2012 <http://abob.libs.uga.edu/bobk/phaeth.html>

Bob Kobres, "A Nickel Pickle: The Problems of Building High-Tech From a Meteoroid Wreck", accessed January 2012 <http://abob.libs.uga.edu/bobk/nicb.html>

James A Marusek, Did a Supernova Cause the Collapse of the Bronze Age Civilisations?" Accessed December 2011 <http://tinyurl.com/c6xue7h>

Timo Niroma, "Evidence of Astronomical Aspects of Mankind's Past and Recent Climate" accessed January 2012 <http://personal.eunet.fi/pp/tilmari/tilmari2.htm#bc2193>

Richard Michael Pasichnyk, "1250-1050 BC -- An Example of an Historical Cycle and the Renewal of Wilderness" <http://www.livingcosmos.com/1250-1050BC.htm>

Barbara Rappengluck, Michael A. Rappengluck, Kord Ernstson, Werner Mayer, Andreas Neumair, Dirk Sudhaus and Ioannis Liritzis, "The fall of Phaethon: a Greco-Roman geomyth preserves the memory of a meteorite impact in Bavaria (south-east Germany)". Accessed January 2012 <http://findarticles.com/p/articles/mi_hb3284/is_324_84/ai_n56365606/>

F Richard Stephenson and Kevin K C Yau, "Astronomical Records in the Chiun-Ch'iu Chronicle", *Journal for the History of Astronomy,* Vol.23. 1992. Accessed January 2012 <http://www.caeno.org/_Nabonassar/pdf/Stephenson_Yau%20Chun%20chiu.pdf>

John Williams, *Observations of comets, from B. C. 611 to A. D. 1640.* Strangeways and Walden: London, 1871. Accessed January 2012 < http:// tinyurl.com/d6ysu35 >

Anne Wright, "Scorpio", Constellations of Words. Accessed January 2012 <http://www.constellationsofwords.com/Constellations/Scorpio.html>

Sun Xiaochun and Jacob Kistemaker, T*he Chinese Sky During The Han.* Brill: New York, 1997.

Zhentao Xu, David W. Pankenier and Yaotiao Jiang. *East Asian Archaeoastronomy.* Gordon and Breach Science Publishers: Amsterdam. 2000.

Perigree Zero, "Proposed Comet Astrophysics", Accessed January 2012 <http://perigeezero.org/treatise/technology/comets/index.html>

8 - WET

"History of Astronomy – Ancient India", ephemeris.com. 2003-4, accessed February 2012, http://ephemeris.com/history/india.html

"Noah's Flood: Dated to May 10th 2807 B.B.", Mathilda's Weird World Weblog. 2009, accessed February 2012 <http://mathildasweirdworldweblog. wordpress.com/2008/10/24/noahs-flood-dated-to-may-10th-2807-bc/>

D S Allan and J B Delair, "When the Earth Nearly Died", Knowledge Computing. 1997, accessed February 2012 http://www.knowledge.co.uk/xxx/cat/earth/index.htm

Andrew Bennett, "Noah's Flood", SunnyOkanagan.com. 1999-2011, accessed February 2012 <http://sunnyokanagan.com/joshua/flood.html>

Nigel Blair, "The Search for Atlantis", Biblioteca Pleyades. 1996, accessed February 2012 <http://www.bibliotecapleyades.net/atlantida_mu/esp_atlantida_6.htm> & <http://www.bibliotecapleyades.net/serpents_dragons/gilgamesh04.htm>

Jno Cook, "The Flood Reconsidered", Recovering the Lost World. 2001-2012, accessed February 2012 <http://saturniancosmology.org/noah.php#fn46>

Lambert Dolphin, "On the Great Flood of Noah", Lambert Dolphin' Library. 1983-2008 accessed February 2012 <http://www.ldolphin.org/flood.shtml>

Alan Dundes (ed.), *The Flood Myth.* University of California Press: Berkeley, 1988.

Louis Ginzberg, "Legends of the Jews", About.com Classic Literature. Accessed February 2012 <http://classiclit.about.com/library/bl-etexts/lginzberg/bl-lginzberg-legends-1-4f.htm>

Alfred Hamori, "The origin of the Sumerians and the great flood", Hungarian Heritage Page. A2004, accessed February 2012 <http://users.cwnet.com/millenia/Sumer-origins.htm>

Frank Humphrey, "The Great Flood and Halloween - A Christian response to Halloween", Free Republic. 1997, accessed February 2012 <http://www. freerepublic.com/focus/f-religion/1012521/posts>

Mark Isaak, "Flood Stories from around the World", Talk Origins Archive. 2002, accessed February 2012 <http://www.talkorigins.org/faqs/flood-myths.html>

Mark Isaak, "Problems with a Global Flood", Talk Origins Archive. 1998, accessed February 2012 <http://www.talkorigins.org/faqs/faq-noahs-ark.html>

Duane E Jeffrey, "Noah's Flood: Modern Scholarship and Mormon Traditions", Sunstone. The Sunshine Educational Federation: Salt Lake City, Utah, October 2004.

Steve Keohane, "The Case for Creationism", *Bible Probe*. Accessed February 2012 <http://bibleprobe.com/creationism.htm>

Munir Ahmed Khan, "Noah's Flood in Bible, Quran and Mesopotamiam Sources". Accessed February 2012 http://www.alislam.org/library/articles/new/NOAH_FLOOD_I.pdf

David Leeming, "Flood", The Oxford Companion to World Mythology. Oxford University Press. Accessed 17 September 2010. <http://www.oxfordreference.com/views/ENTRY.html?subview=Main&entry=t208.e567>

R Cedric Leonard, "The Mayan Flood", *Quest for Atlantis*. Accessed February 2012 <http://www.atlantisquest.com/Chum_l.html>

David Livingston, "The Date of Noah's Flood", *Ancient Days*. 2003, accessed February 2012 <http://davelivingston.com/flooddate.htm>

David Livingston, "A Universal Flood: 3000 BC ", Ancient Days. 2003, accessed February 2012 <http://davelivingston.com/universalflood.htm>

Ellen Lloyd, *Voices from Legendary Times*. iUniverse: Lincoln, NE, 2005.

Dave Moore, "Supernovae, Supernova Remnants and Young Earth Creationism FAQ", Talk Origins Archive. 2001, accessed February 2012 <http://www.talkorigins.org/faqs/supernova/>

J Osgood, "The Date of Noah's Flood", answersingenesis.org. 2012, accessed February 2012 <http://www.answersingenesis.org/articles/cm/v4/n1/date-of-noahs-flood>

Tom Pickett, "Noah's Flood, The Genesis Files. 2005, accessed February 2012 <http://www.genesisfiles.com/Flood.htm>

John P Pratt, "Astronomical Witnesses of the Great Flood", JohnPratt.com. 2003, accessed February 2012 <http://www.johnpratt.com/items/docs/lds/meridian/2003/deluge.html>

Robert B Stacey- Judd, Atlantis: Mother of Empires. Adventures Unlimited Press: Illinois, 1939.

James Ussher, *Annals of the World*. London, 1658.

William Whiston, *A New Theory of the Earth*. London, 1755.

9 - Knocking on Heaven's Door

Richard Hinchley Allen, *Star Names: Their Lore and Meaning*. Dover Publications: London, 1889/1963.

Aristotle, *Meteorology*. Accessed February 2012 <http://classics.mit.edu/Aristotle/meteorology.1.i.html>

Authentic Maya, "Maya Astronomy", Authentic Maya. 2005, accessed February 2012 <http://www.authenticmaya.com/maya_astronomy.htm>

Kelley Coblentz Bautch, *A Study of the Geography of 1 Enoch 17-19*. Brill: Leiden NL, 2003.

Martin Bulgerin, "Precession", BioPsciences Institute. 2003, accessed February 2012 <http://members.bitstream.net/bunlion/bpi/precess6.html>

Sadaputa Dasa, "Astronomy and the Antiquity of Vedic Civilization", Krishna.com. 2002-2012, access February 2012 <http://www.krishna.com/astronomy-and-antiquity-vedic-civilization>

Gary A David, The Orion Zone: Ancient Star Cities of the American Southwest. Adventures Unlimited Press: Illinois, 2007.

Thomas Karl Dietrich ,"The Milky Way", *The Culture of Astronomy*. 2005, accessed February 2012. <http://www.cosmomyth.com/milky_way.html>

Penny Drayton, "In Heaven as on Earth", *Royal roads and the Milky Way*. 1995, accessed February 2012 <http://www.indigogroup.co.uk/edge/Royalrds.htm>

W H Duignan, *Notes on Staffordshire Place Names*. Oxford University Press: Oxford, 1902.

John David Ebert and John Lobell, "On Gilgamesh" Cinema Cultural Discourse. 2004-10, accessed February 2012 <http://cinemadiscourse.com/cultural/?p=340>

Alfred Edersheim, *History of the Jewish Nation After the Destruction of Jerusalem Under Titus,* Aberdeen 1856.

Dana Facaros and Michael Pauls, "Northern Spain: The Pilgrimage to Santiago", Travel Guides. 2009, accessed January 2012 < http://facarospauls.com/Spain/Northern+Spain/>

Andrei Dorian Gheorghe and Alastair McBeath, "Gheonoaia & Scorpia: More Romanian Dragons", Cosmo Poetry. 1998, accessed February 2012 <http://www.cosmopoetry.ro/Romanian%20Astrohumanism%207/Pages/romanian_astrohumanism_VII-4.htm>

Manley P Hall, The Secret Teachings of All Ages. 1928, accessed February 2012 <http://www.sacred-texts.com/eso/sta/sta12.htm>

Andres Kuperjanov, "Names in Estonian Folk Astronomy". Accessed February 2012 < www.folklore.ee/folklore/vol22/milkyway.pdf>

Lunarium, *Piers Plowman.* Accessed February 2012 <http://www.luminarium.org/medlit/plowman.htm>

Fiona Macleod (William Sharp), "The Milky Way, Where the Forest Murmers." Sundown Shores: 1998-2001, accessed February 2012 <http://www.sundown.pair.com/SundownShores/Volume_VI/ForestMurmers/milky%20way.htm>

James L Matterer, "Pilgrims Passing to and Fro", The Lives & Times of the Canterbury Tales Pilgrims. Accessed February 2012 <http://www.godecookery.com/pilgrims/pilgrm04.htm>

Paul Perov, "The Galactic Alignment". Accessed February 2012 <http://pperov.angelfire.com/galactic.html>

Vivian E Robson, *Fixed Stars and Constellations in Astrology*. Astrology Center of America: New York, 2005.

Giorgio de Santillana and Hertha von Dechend, *Hamlet's Mill: an Essay on Myth and the Frame of Time*. Godine: Boston: 1977.

Linda Schele and Khristaan de Villela, "Creation, Cosmos and the Imagery of Palenque and Coban". University of Texas: 1992, accessed February 2012 <www.mesoweb.com/pari/publications/rt10/creation.pdf>

Souled Out, "Aldebaran: The Eye of Illumination", Souled Out. Accessed February 2012 <http://souledout.org/cosmology/highlights/aldebaran.html>

Watch Unto Prayer, "Taurus: Orion the Stargate", The False Gospel in the Stars. Accessed February 2012 <http://watch.pair.com/taurus.html>

Jan Wicherink and Aaron Parlier, "Gates of the Sun", Key of Solomon. 2008, accessed February 2012 <http://www.keyofsolomon.org/gatesOfTheSun.php>

Jan Wicherink, Souls of Distortion. 2006, accessed January 2012 <http://www.soulsofdistortion.nl>

Anne Wright "Milky Way", Constellations of Words. 2008, accessed February 2012 http://www.constellationsofwords.com/stars/milky_way.html

Anne Wright "Scorpio", Constellations of Words. 2008, accessed February 2012 <http://www.constellationsofwords.com/Constellations/Scorpio.html>

10 · CLIMBING UPWARDS

Hartley Burr Alexander. The Mythology of All Races. Volume: 10. Cooper Square Publishers: New York, 1964.

Ed Cochrane. "Ladder to Heaven". Accessed January 2012 <http://www.thelivingmoon.com/42stargate/03files/Ladder_Heaven.html>

Tom and Nita Horn. "Stargates of the Gods". Anomalos Publishing. Accessed January 2012 < http://www.ahrimangate.com/excerpt162.htm>

Allan Macgillivray III, The Venus Calendar Observatory at Aztec New Mexico. Author House: Bloomington, Indiana, 2010.

MaverickScience.com. "The Stairway to Heaven". Accessed February 2012 <http://www.maverickscience.com/mars-stairway-to-heaven.htm>

Jan Wicherink. "2012 Freemason Revelations". Accessed January 2012 <http://www.soulsofdistortion.nl/2012_freemasons_revelations.html>

11 · I FOUND THAT ESSENCE RARE

Syamsuddin Arif, "The Universe as a System: Ibn Sina's Cosmology Revisited", Islam & Science Volume: 7. Issue: 2. Center for Islam & Science: 2009.

Jeff Bary and Deborah Parker, "Astronomy in the Divine Comedy", The World of Dante. Accessed March 2012 <http://www.worldofdante.org/astro1.html>

H Butterfield, The Origins of Modern Science: 1300-1800. Macmillan: New York. 1957.

Julia Ching, The Religious Thought of Chu Hsi. Oxford University Press: New York, 2000.

A C Crombie, Augustine to Galileo: The History of Science, A.D. 400- 1650. William Heinemann: Melbourne, 1952.

A C Crombie (Ed.), Historical Studies in the Intellectual, Social, and Technical Conditions for Scientific Discovery and Technical Invention, from Antiquity to the Present. Basic Books: New York, 1963.

Philip M. Dauber and Richard A. Muller, The Three Big Bangs: Comet Crashes, Exploding Stars, and the Creation of the Universe. Perseus Books: Cambridge, MA, 1996.

Harvie Ferguson, The Science of Pleasure: Cosmos and Psyche in the Bourgeois World View. Routledge: London, 1990.

Stephen Gaukroger, Descartes' System of Natural Philosophy. Cambridge University Press: Cambridge, 2002.

Jeremiah Genest, "The Heavens", Ars Magica Portal. 1998, accessed March 2012 <http://www.granta.demon.co.uk/arsm/jg/heaven.html>

Manly P Hall, The Sacred teachings of all Ages. 1928, accessed March 2012 <http://www.sacred-texts.com/eso/sta/sta03.htm>

John F Hawley and Katherine A Holcomb, Foundations of Modern Cosmology. Oxford University Press: New York, 1998.

Albert Van Helden, "Ptolemaic System", Connexions. 2004, accessed March 2012 <http://cnx.org/content/m11943/latest/>

Francis R Johnson, Thought in Renaissance England: A Study of the English Scientific Writing from 1500 to 1645. Johns Hopkins Press: Baltimore, MD, 1937.

David Lindberg, Science in the Middle Ages. University of Chicago Press: Chicago, 1980.

Steven Nadler, Spinoza's Heresy: Immortality and the Jewish Mind. Clarendon Press: Oxford, 2001.

Jeff Bary and Deborah Parker, "Astronomy in the Divine Comedy", The World of Dante. Accessed March 2012 <http://www.worldofdante.org/astro1.html>

Janet Radcliffe Richards, Human Nature after Darwin: A Philosophical Introduction. Routledge: London, 2000.

Adi Setia, "Fakhr Al-Din Al-Razi on Physics and the Nature of the Physical World: A Preliminary Survey", Islam & Science. Volume: 2. Issue: 2. Center for Islam & Science: 2004.

Adam Smith, Essays on Philosophical Subjects. Oxford University Press: Oxford, 1980.

Michael Windelspecht, Groundbreaking Scientific Experiments, Inventions and Discoveries of the 17th Century. Greenwood Press: Westport, CT, 2002.

Alice's Medieval, "Advent". Accessed February 2012 <http://mw.mcmaster.ca/scriptorium/alice_site/advent_more_end.html>

John Brand and Henry Ellis, Observations on Popular Antiquities Chiefly Illustrating the Origin of our Vulgar Customs, Ceremonies, and Supersititions. Chatto and Windus: New York, 1900.

Robert Chambers, Chamber's Book of Days. 1869, accessed February 2012 http://www.thebookofdays.com/about_bod.htm

Fisheaters, "Feast of St. Martin". Accessed February 2012 <http://fisheaters.com/customstimeafterpentecost15.html>

J G R Forlong, Rivers of life, or, Sources and streams of the faiths of man in all lands : showing the evolution of faiths from the rudest symbolisms to the latest spiritual developments. London,1883, accessed February 2012 <http://www.archive.org/stream/riversoflife01forlrich/riversoflife01forlrich_djvu.txt>

Frazier, James George, Sir. The Golden Bough, Volume II, Part IV. Macmillan: New York, 1922.

Mall Hiiemäe, "Souls' Visiting Time in the Estonian Folk calendar", Estonian Folklore. Accessed March 2012 <http://www.folklore.ee/rl/pubte/ee/usund/ingl/hiiemae.html>

Ronald Hutton, Stations of the Sun: A History of the Ritual Year in Britain. Oxford University Press: Oxford, 1996.

RG Haliburton, The Festival of the Dead. Journal of the Royal Astronomical Society of Canada, Vol. 15. 1921, accessed February 2012 <1921JRASC..15...12H>http://adsabs.harvard.edu/full/1920JRASC..14..292H#http://articles.adsabs.harvard.edu//full/1921JRASC..15...12H/0000014.000.html

Frank Joseph, The Destruction of Atlantis: Compelling Evidence of the Sudden Fall of the Legendary Civilization. Bear & Co: Vermont, 2002.

D M Murdock, S Acharya and N W Barker, The 2010 Astrotheology Calendar. Astrotheology Press: 2009.

Rev. R. Smiddy, The Druids, &c., of Ireland. Kelly: Dublin, 1873.

Charles Piazzi Smyth, Life and Work at the Great Pyramid During the Months of January, February, March and April A.D. 1865. Edinburgh, 1867.

Maya Magee Sutton and Nicholas Mann, Druid Magic: The Practice of Celtic Wisdom. Llewellyn Publications: 2000.

Robert Poole, "'Give us our eleven days!': calendar reform in eighteenth-century England". Oxford University Press: 1995, accessed February 2012 <http://findarticles.com/p/articles/mi_m2279/is_n149/_17782422/?tag=content;col1>

what-when-how,"Dardanus To Diodorus Siculus". Accessed February 2012 <http://what-when-how.com/the-atlantis/dardanus-to-diodorus-siculus/>

Don Wildgrube. The Festival Wheel.1993, accessed February 2012 <http://www.ladyoftheearth.com/sabbats/festival-wheel.txt>

American Library Institute Papers and Proceedings, Chicago, 1917. Accessed February 2012 <http://www.archive.org/stream/papersandprocee00instgoog/papersandprocee00instgoog_djvu.txt>

Michael David Bailey, Magic and Superstition in Europe. Rowman and Littlefield: Maryland, 2007.

Bonnie Blackburn and Leofranc Holford-Strevens, The Oxford Companion to the Year. Oxford University Press: Oxford, 1999.

Archibald Bower, Historia litteraria. London, 1732.

Robert Chambers, Chamber's Book of Days. 1869, accessed February 2012 <http://www.thebookofdays.com/about_bod.htm>

Digital Collections Program, The Calendar and the Cloister. McGill University, 2007, accessed February 2012 <http://digital.library.mcgill.ca/ms-17/index.htm>

John C Hirsh, "Fate, Faith and Paradox: Medieval Unlucky Days as a Context for 'Wytte Hath Wondyr'", Medium Aevum. Volume: 66. Issue: 2. Society for the Study of Mediaeval Languages and Literature: 1997.

Hermann Hunger and David Edwin Pingree, Astral Sciences in Mesopotamia. Koninklije Brill NV: Leiden, NL,1999.

Morris Jastrow Jr, Hebrew and Babylonian Traditions: The Haskell Lectures, Delivered at Oberlin College in 1913. Charles Scribner's Sons: New York, 1914.

Samuel Macauley Jackson (Ed.), The New Schaff-Herzog Encyclopedia of Religious Knowledge. Volume: 10. Funk and Wagnalls: New York, 1911.

Ulla Susanne Koch, "Concepts and Perception of Time in Mesopotamian Divination". Paper given at the Rencontre Assyriologique International 2010, accessed February 2012, <http://ku-dk.academia.edu/UllaSusanneKoch/Papers/485464/Concepts_and_Perception_of_Time_in_Mesopotamian_Divination>

Robert Means Lawrence, The Magic of the Horse-Shoe. Houghton, Mifflin and Company: Boston and New York, 1898. Accessed February 2012 <sacred-texts.com/etc/mhs/mhs52.htm>

John Scott Lucas, Astrology and Numerology in Medieval and Early Modern Catalonia. Koninklije Brill NV: Leiden, NL, 2003.

Online Library of Liberty, A Balade of Compleynt, Geoffrey Chaucer, The Complete Works of Geoffrey Chaucer, vol. 1 (Romaunt of the Rose, Minor Poems) [1899]. Accessed February 2012, <http://oll.libertyfund.org/?option=com_staticxt&staticfile=show.php%3Ftitle=1989&chapter=128995&layout=html&Itemid=27>

Laszlo Sandor Chardonnes, Anglo Saxon Prognostics. Koninklijke Brill: Leiden, NL, 2007.

P. Le Page Renouf, Lectures on the Origin and Growth of Religion as Illustrated by the Religion of Ancient Egypt. Delivered in May and June, 1879. Williams and Norgate: London, 1884.

E G Richards, Mapping Time: The Calendar and Its History. Oxford University Press: Oxford, 1999.

Bernice Glatzer Rosenthal, The Occult in Russian and Soviet Culture. Cornell University Press: Ithaca, NY, 1997.

Robert Steele, "Dies Aegyptiaci", PRSM 12, Section of the History of Medicine Supplement, 108-121. Accessed February 2012, < www.ncbi.nlm. nih.gov/pmc/articles/.../pdf/procrsmed01131-0383.pdf>

Sacha Stern, Calendar and Community: A History of the Jewish Calendar. Oxford University Press: Oxford, 2001.

Roland De Vaux (Trans. John McHugh), Ancient Israel: Its Life and Institutions. McGraw-Hill: New York, 1961.

Merriam Webster, The Merriam-Webster new book of word histories. Merriam Webster: USA, 1991.

Theodore Otto Wedel, Medieval Attitude Towards Astrology Particularly in England. Kessinger Publishing, 2003.

14 - OUR HOUSE

Richard Hinckley Allen , Star Names Their Lore and Meaning . 1963, accessed March 2012 <http://penelope.uchicago.edu/Thayer/E/Gazetteer/ Topics/astronomy/_Texts/secondary/ALLSTA/Lunar_Mansions*.html>

Gauranga Nath Banerjee, Hellenism in Ancient India. Munshi Ram Manohar Lal: Delhi, 1961.

Giuseppe Bezza, "Du Calendrier naturel à l'Astrologie", CURA. 2000, accessed January 2012 <http://cura.free.fr/quinq/04bezza.html>

Margaret L. Ionides and Stephen A. Ionides, Stars and Men. Bobbs-Merrill: Indianapolis, 1939.

Arthyr Chadbourne, "The Lunar Mansion", TheSunsetChart.com. 2008, accessed February 2012, <http://www.kaldu.com/lunarmansion.html>

Coching Chu, The Origin of Twenty-Eight Mansions in Astronomy" Popular Astronomy, Vol. 55, p.62. Accessed February 2012, <http://adsabs. harvard.edu/full/1947PA.....55...62C>

Jim A Cornwell, "Manazil and its connection to Mazzaroth", Mazzaroth. 1995, accessed February 2012 <http://www.mazzaroth.com/Introduction/ ManazilDefined.htm>

G T Garratt (Ed.), The Legacy of India. Clarendon Press: Oxford, 1937.

Aiyer B V Kamesvara. "The Lunar Zodiac in the Brāhman☒as." Indian Antiquary 48. June 1919.

Alan Leo, The Astrologer's Magazine. 1894, accessed February 2012 <http://www.archive.org/stream/astrologersmaga00unkngoog#page/n235/ mode/1up>

Neil Mann, "The Mansions of the Moon." Accessed February 2012, http:// www.yeatsvision.com/Mansions.html

Thomas Maurice, The history of Hindostan: its arts, and its sciences, as connected with the history of the other great empires of Asia, during the most ancient periods of the world, with numerous illustrated engravings, Volume 1. W. Bulmer and W. Nicol: 1820.

Weixing Niu, "Astronomy in the Sutras Translated into Chinese", Studies in the History of Medicine & Science, Vol.XV, No.1-2, New Series. 1997/1998, accessed March 2012 < http://shc2000.sjtu.edu.cn/0406/astronomy.htm>

E G Richards, The Calendar and Its History. Oxford University Press: Oxford, 1999.

George Saliba, A History of Arabic Astronomy. NYU Press: New York, 1995

Edward C Sachau, Alberuni's India: an account of the religion, philosophy, and literature. Trubner: London, 1888.

Nagendra Kumar Singh, Encyclopaedia of Hinduism. Centre for International Religious Studies: Anmol Publications, 2002.

Daniel Varisco, "The Origin of the anwā' in Arab Tradition", Studia Islamica No. 74, pp. 5-28. Maisonneuve & Larose: 1991.

Daniel Varisco,"Islamic Folk Astronomy", Astronomy Across Cultures. 2000.

Daniel Varisco, "Stars and Texts in Arabia", Archaeoastronomy & Ethnoastronomy News, Number 16, June Solstice, 1995.

15 - HANDY

Astrostar.ru, accessed December 2011, <http://palmistry.astrostar.ru/line/25958.html >

"A Table of Palmistry from Saunders",The Astrologer's Magazine and Philosophical Miscellany, Volume 1. London, February 1792.

Nathan Bailey, An Universal Etymological English Dictionary. London, 1737.

Egbert Buys, A New and Complete Dictionary of Terms of Art. Amsterdam, 1768.

George Crabb, Universal Technological Dictionary, Baldwin, Cradock & Joy: London, 1851.

Mrs J B Dal, Indian Palmistry. Theosophical Publishing Society: Madras, 1895.

Grillot de Givry (Tr. J Courtenay Locke), Witchcraft, Magic & Alchemy, Dover Occult: 2009.

Randle Holmes, The Academy of Armory. London, 1688.

Christopher Jones, "Chiromantia Theorica Practica", The History of Hand Reading. At Johnny Fincham, Palmistry, accessed November 2011 ,<http://www.johnnyfincham.com/history/rothmann.htm>

Christopher Jones, "Physiognomie, Chiromancie, Metoposcopie", The History of Hand Reading. At Johnny Fincham, Palmistry, accessed November 2011, <http://www.johnnyfincham.com/history/rothmann.htm>

Nicholas Gyer, The English Phlebotomy. London, 1592.

Aaron Hill, The plain dealer: being select essays on several curious subjects. London, 1724.

John ab Indagine, (Tr. Fabian Withers) Introductiones Apostelesmaticae. London, 1651.

W Pickering, The Gentleman's Magazine. Volume 10, 1838.

Johannes Rothmann, (Tr. George Whaton), Chiromantiae Theorica Practica. London, 1652.

Ebenezer Sibly, The Conjurer's Magazine. London: August 1791.

Heasim Sul, Hope and fear in Seventeenth Century England: Richard Saunders' Chiromantic Textbook. Yonsei University: Seoul, Korea, 2009.

Johannes Taisnier, Opus Mathematicum. Cologne, 1562.

William George Waters, A Biographical Study of Jerome Cardan. Lawrence and Bullen: London, 1898. Accessed November 2011 <http://www.gutenberg.org/files/19600/19600-8.txt>

Zeno.org, accessed November 2011, http://www.zeno.org/Literatur/M/Br%C3%A4uner,+Johann+Jacob/Werk/Physicalisch-+und+Historisch-Er%C3%B6rterte+Curiositaeten/32.+Von+der+Chiromantia

16 - STARGATE

Aux Mailles Godefroy, "Via Combusta", accessed 20 November 2011 <http://www.auxmaillesgodefroy.com/via_combusta>

James Spottiswode, "A Possible Discovery Regarding ESP" Society for Scientific Exploration. Accessed November 2011 <http://www.remoteviewers.com/htms/updated/info/general_rv/sidereal.htm>

17 - BUT WHAT DOES IT MEAN?

Astrology Notes, Via Combusta". Astrology Notes: 2006, accessed February 2012 <http://astrologynotes.org/wiki/Via_Combusta>

Nathan Bailey, An Universal Etymological English Dictionary. Thomas Cox: London, 1787.

Joseph Blagrave, Astrological Practice of Physick, London, 1671.

László Sándor Chardonnens Anglo-Saxon Prognostics, 900-1100: Study and Texts. Brill: Leiden, Boston, 2007.

Paul Christian, History and Practice of Magic. Kessinger: 1994. p. 582.

Henry Coley, Centiloquium of Hermes Trismegistus in Clavis Astrologiae Elimata (Key to the Whole Art of Astrology). London: 1676.

Nicholas Culpeper, Opus astrologicum. London: Moone & Steph, 1654.

Dorotheus (Tr. David Pingree), Carmen Astrologicum. Ascella Publications: London, 1993.

William Eland, A Tutor to Astrology. London: 1694.

Archie Dunlop, Elnu. Accessed December 2011 <http://www.elnu.com/blog/archives/19>

William Eland, A Tutor to Astrology. London, 1694.

John Fage, Speculum Aegrotorum. London, 1606 .

John Gadbury, The Doctrine of Nativities & Horary Questions. Giles Calvert: London, 1658.

John Gadbury, Nauticum Astrologicum or The Astrologer's Seaman. London, 1660.

Grillot de Givry (Tr. J Courtenay Locke), Witchcraft, Magic & Alchemy, Dover Occult: 2009.

Nicholas Gyer, The English Phlebotomy. London, 1592.

John M Hansen, "Business Astrology 2008-08-12"AFA. Accessed January 2012 <http://www.astrologers.com/news/view-article.php?article_id=10>

Syed Athar Husain and SH Rizvi, SH Islamic Marriage A Handbook for Young Muslims. Mumbai: World Islamic Network, 2001.

Marc Edmund Jones, Horary Astrology. Shambala: London, 1975.

Lashtal, Home of the Aleister Crowley Society. 1998-2002, accessed December 2011 <www.lashtal.com/nuke/PNphpBB2-printview-t-1205-start-0.phtm>

William Lilly, Christian Astrology. London:1647.

Middle English Text on Planting and Grafting in Cambridge, Trinity College, O.5.26.

John Middleton, Practical Astrology. London: 1679.

Robert Means Lawrence, The Magic of the Horse-Shoe. Houghton, Mifflin and Company: Boston and New York, 1898. Accessed 20 November 2012 <sacred-texts.com/etc/mhs/mhs52.htm>

Joseph Moxon, Mathematicks Made Easy. London 1679.

John Partridge, Mikropanastron, or an Astrological Vade Mecum, briefly Teaching the whole Art of Astrology - viz., Questions, Nativities, with all its parts, and the whole Doctrine of Elections never so comprised nor compiled before, &c. London: William Bromwich, 1679.

William Ramesey, Astrologia Restaurata, London, 1653.

Vivian Robson, Electional Astrology. JP Lippincott: London, 1937.

Richard Saunders, Astrological Judgement and Practice of Physick. London, 1671.

Ebenezer Sibly, A New and Complete Illustration of the Celestial Science of Astrology. 1795.

WJ Simmonite, The Complete Arcana of Astral Philosophy. London, 1890.

WJ Simmonite, Horary Astrology. John Story: London, 1896.

Diana Stone, "Questions and Answers", The Fraser Valley Astrological Guild. Accessed January 2012 <http://www.astrologyguild.com/horary1.htm>

Richard Thomson, Tales of an Antiquary. London: Colburn & R. Bentley: London, 1828.

WilliamThrasher, Jubar Astrologicum or a True Astrological Guide. London:1671.

University of Glasgow. "Middle English Text on Planting and Grafting in Cambridge, Trinity College, O.5.26", Medical Treatises England: c.1475-1500. <http://special.lib.gla.ac.uk/exhibns/month/may2006.html> (Accessed 30 November 2011.

Nicholas de Vore, Encyclopedia of Astrology. Astrology Classics Publishing: New York, 2005 (1947 facsimile).